PAUL OF TARSUS

AN ENIGMA ENSHROUDED IN A MYSTERY

An investigation

by
Arthur Woods

Published in Great Britain in 2005 by Arthur Woods

Copyright © Arthur Woods, 2005

Designed and typeset by Andrew Haig & Associates

Printed and bound in Great Britain by Antony Rowe Limited

The moral right of the authors has been asserted.

A CIP catalogue record for this book is available from
the British Library.

ISBN 09546773-1-5

COVER IMAGE
'Paul on Road to Damascus', Doré, 1865

A DEDICATION

To the martyrs who died unflinchingly for their faith.

To those who were killed in defence of their faith.

To the poor who were killed anyway,
because they always are.

ACKNOWLEDGEMENTS

To Cindy Foster who put the book on the word processor, and prepared the floppy disc. To Mike Foster, who made many journeys ferrying crude manuscripts from Lindfield to Maidstone, and typed manuscripts back to me. To the friends, startled by what I was writing, telling me that St Paul would be a 'turn-off', and without whose discouragement this book might not have reached the printers. And to my wife, Kay Woods, who proofread and corrected spelling and grammatical errors.

CONTENTS

A SELECTED BIBLIOGRAPHY

Bible   Old Testament King James' Version

Bible   New Testament King James' Version

Antiquities of the Jews   Josephus

Destruction of the Jews   Josephus

Masada   Yigael Yadin

Decline and Fall of the Roman Empire   Edward Gibbon

The Koran   N. J. Dawood Version

A History of the Arab Peoples   Albert Hourani

Introducing the New Testament   John Drane

The Bible as History   Werner Keller

In the Footsteps of Saint Paul   Wolfgang Pax

Acts of the Apostles   Richard Wallace and Wynne Williams

Paul   A.N. Wilson

Montaillou   Emmanuel Le Roy Ladurie

The Unauthorised Version   Robin Lane-Fox

History of Christianity   Paul Johnson

The Black Death   Philip Ziegler

Julian   Gore Vidal

The Middle East   Bernard Lewis

The Bible Atlas   Times of London Edition

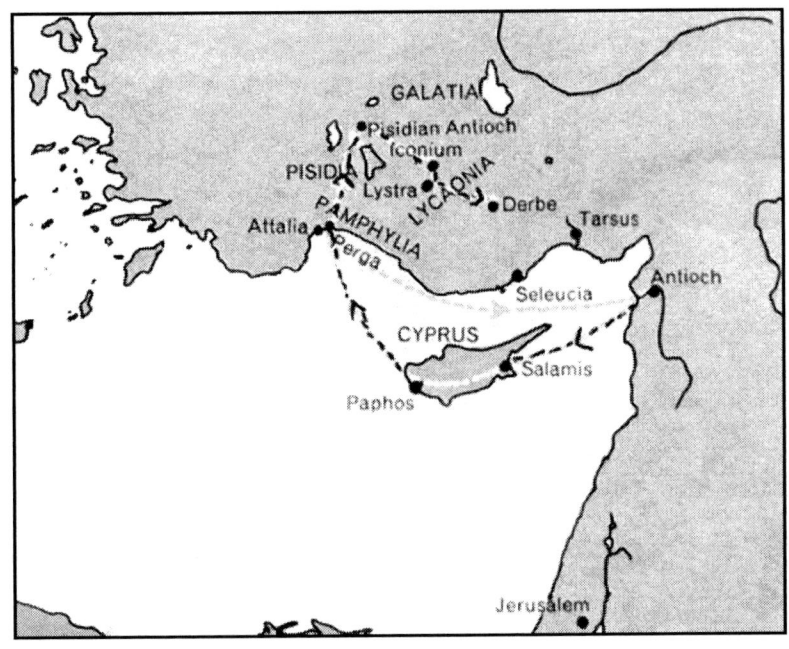

PAUL'S FIRST MISSIONARY JOURNEY

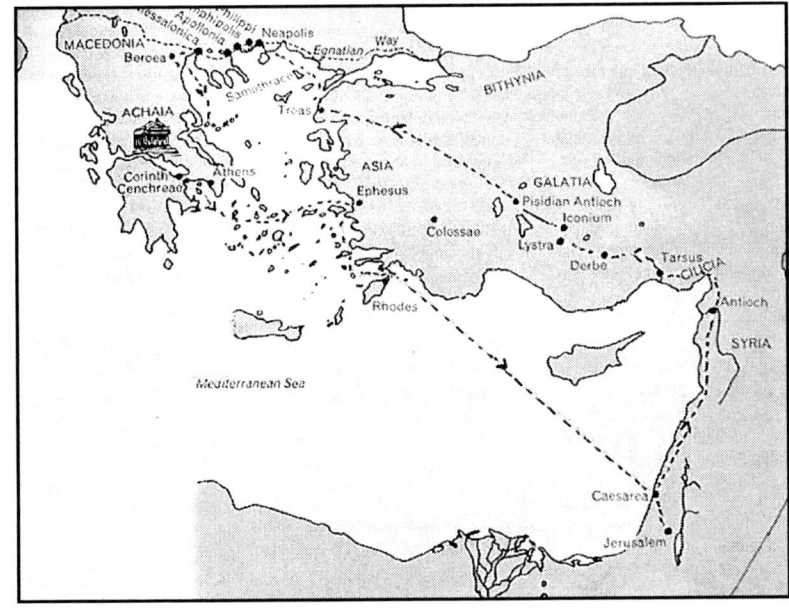

PAUL'S SECOND MISSIONARY JOURNEY

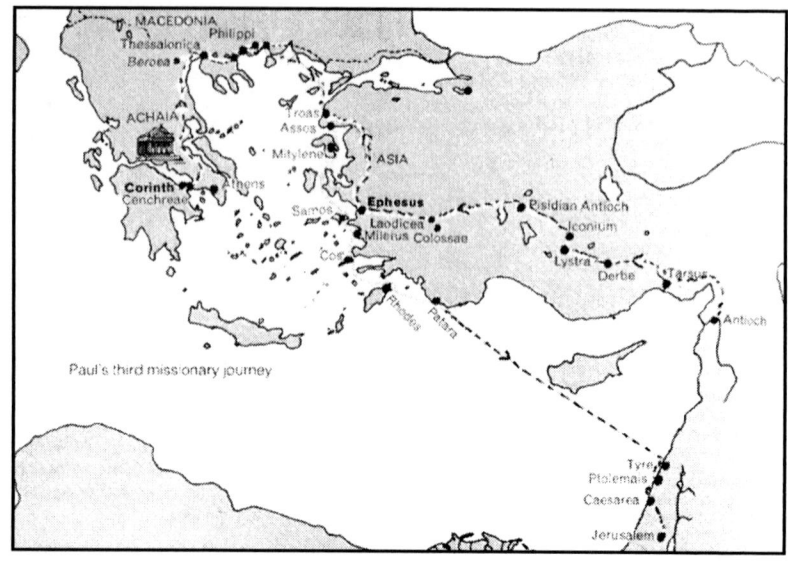

PAUL'S THIRD MISSIONARY JOURNEY

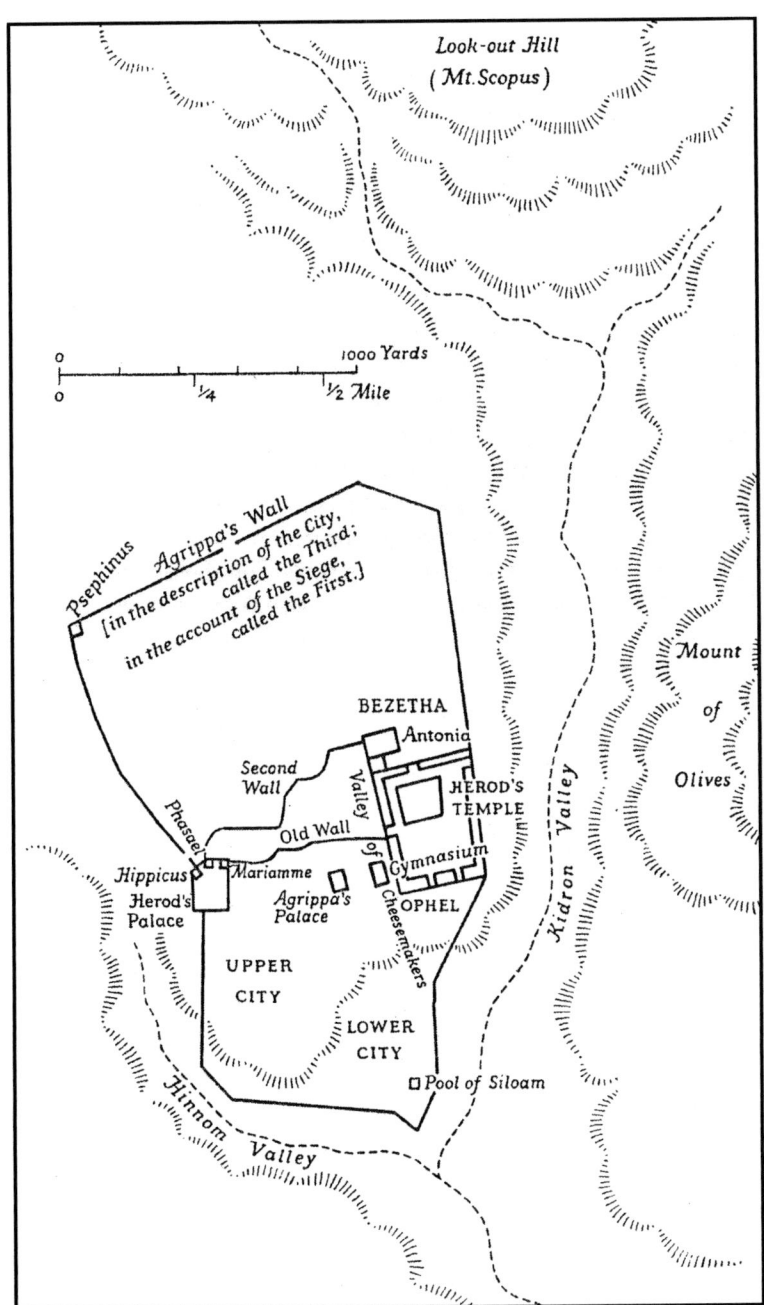

Look-out Hill
(Mt. Scopus)

1000 Yards

¼   ½ Mile

Psephinus

Agrippa's Wall
[in the description of the City, called the Third; in the account of the Siege, called the First.]

BEZETHA

Antonia

Second Wall

Valley

HEROD'S TEMPLE

Mount

of

Olives

Phasael

Old Wall

Gymnasium

Hippicus

Mariamme

Herod's Palace

Agrippa's Palace

of Cheesemakers

OPHEL

Kidron Valley

UPPER CITY

LOWER CITY

Pool of Siloam

Hinnom Valley

JERUSALEM IN 70 A.D.

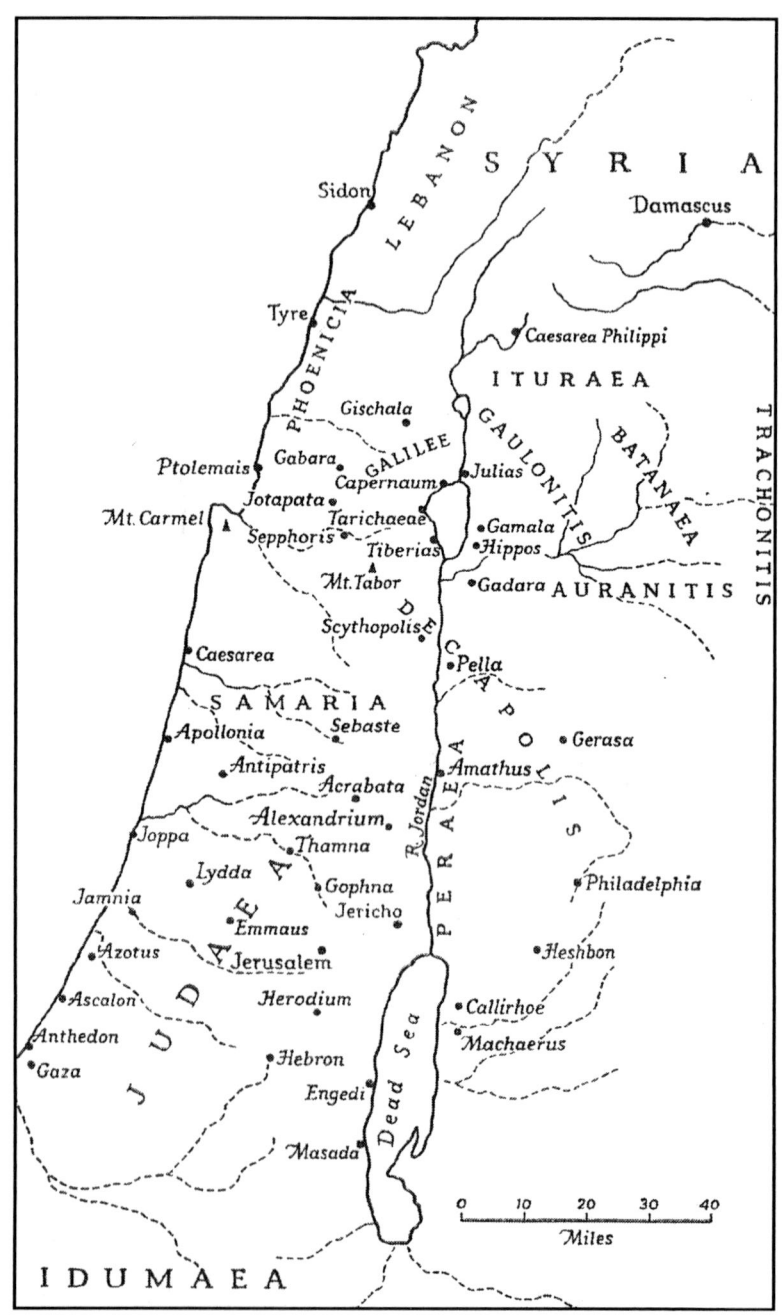

PALESTINE IN THE FIRST CENTUARY A.D.

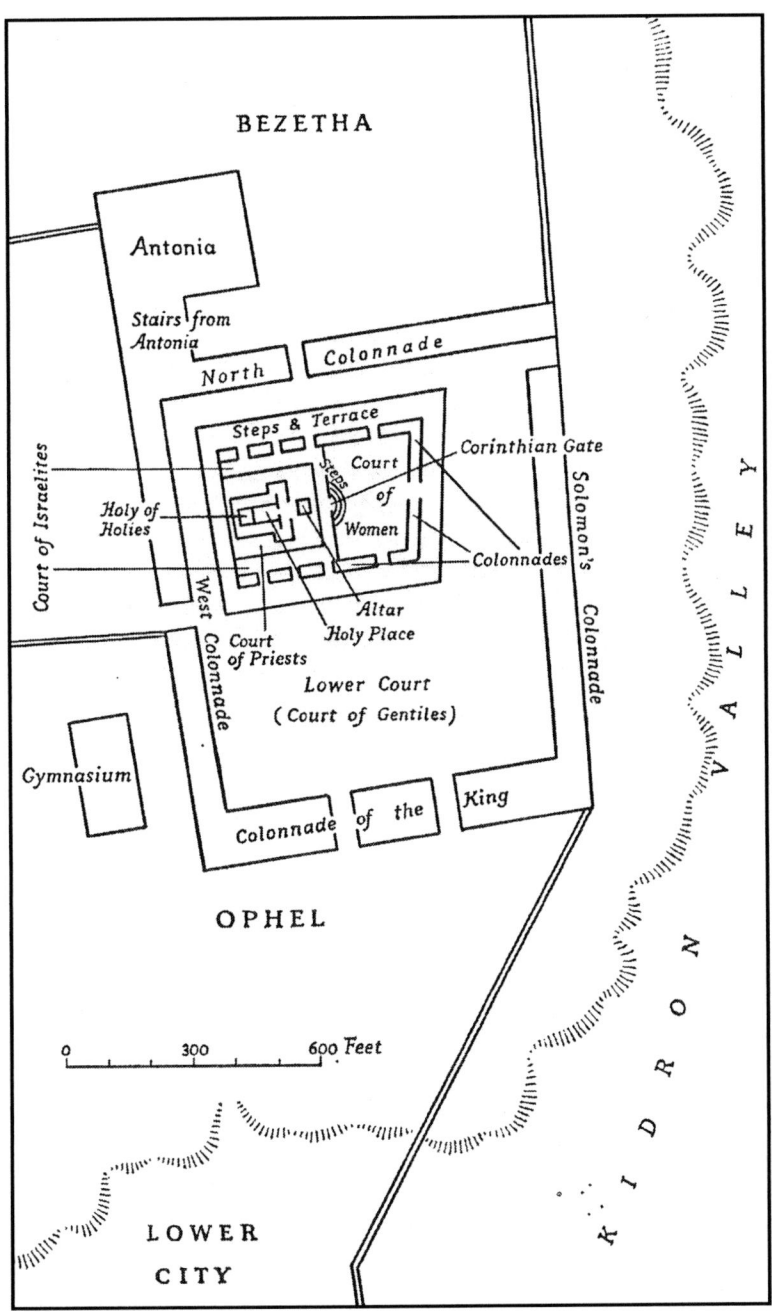

BEZETHA

Antonia

Stairs from
Antonia

North   Colonnade

Steps & Terrace

Court of Israelites

Holy of
Holies

Court
of
Women

Corinthian Gate

Solomon's Colonnade

West Colonnade

Court
of Priests

Altar
Holy Place

Colonnades

Lower Court
(Court of Gentiles)

Gymnasium

Colonnade of the King

OPHEL

VALLEY

0   300   600 Feet

KIDRON

LOWER
CITY

HEROD'S TEMPLE

1

PROLOGUE

At the height of the Summer in 1961 I went to to the Middle East on behalf of my American employers. It was my idea to go and they, in the American way, backed me. Over a four weeks' period I travelled across Israel, Egypt, Turkey and Greece making a technical, commercial and, in some ways, a political survey to determine whether or not there was a market for my company's heavy industrial plant. If so, it would be my job to plan, market and sell it.

All those countries belong historically to the Biblical era and, earlier, to pagan and other practices which, like it or not, played a role in the emergence of Judaism, Christianity and, by no means least, Islam. The heavy hand of history had held them in thrall for centuries and superstition, religious mayhem and wars, not to mention lassitude induced by fatalism, climate and disease held back developments in social, intellectual and scientific fields. At least that is how the puritanical Protestant peoples of the North regarded them.

I travelled the coastal road to Tyre and Sidon; 'The Way of the Sea' as it was called by the armies of Assyria and Persia on their way to conquer Egypt and also, of course, by Abraham and his nomadic tribe as they wandered from Ur of the Chaldees to the land of Canaan; then from Tel Aviv, ancient Joppa, the sixty miles to Jerusalem, flanked by the sunburnt hills pierced by rocky outcrops of white stone with Palestinian villages on the hilltops. I motored the desert road from Eilat and adjacent Jordanian Aqaba across a barren wilderness of sand and shale with the mountains of Ruth's Moab to the East and Moses' Sinai to the West. These roads struck me with awe. There was a silence in the savage terrain which Jacob and his twelve sons would have recognised. The black tents of goat hair and camel skins, shelter for the Bedouin with their flocks of scrawny sheep and goats would have been a familiar sight to the traveller in the time of Jesus. Then, a few years later on a cold Winter's day, I stood with my back to the tawdry and pretentiously named Manger Square in Bethlehem looking at the low snow spattered hills outside the town and I should have been lacking in sentience if that passage in St.Luke about the shepherds guarding their sheep at the time of Jesus had not come to mind.

After my work in Israel I flew over the equally barren and seemingly waterless expanse of Turkish Anatolia and there were few signs of habitation or verdant pastures in the hitherto Graeco Roman provinces of Cilicia, Capadocia, Galatia or Pisidia. Again I had this weird creepy feeling of being in touch with the dramatic events which were played out nearly 2000 years earlier under the tyrannical rule of Rome in the provinces of Palestine, Greece and the Eastern Mediterranean lands. In the towns there was no such feeling as they looked, and felt, like the dusty ramshackle towns of the Balkans.

In the third week of my tour I encountered the most haunting experience of all. Before dawn I left my hotel in the centre of Athens on a morning in July 1961 and walked down Vass Georgiou Street, taking one of the several left turns from which the Acropolis was visible, and to which I was walking, so that I could be alone when the sun rose in the East. Today you couldn't do that: the Acropolis is closed all night to protect the site from the hordes of tourists. I clambered everywhere and wondered at everything.

Finally I stood on the jutting spur called the Areopagus, better known as the Hill of Mars, from which St. Paul is said to have addressed a gathering of Athenians. At five in the morning, the air still warm from the previous day, the hand of history seemed to touch me. On this spot St.Paul had stood in AD49/50, and from that moment, that seminal moment, rarely a month passed without some fleeting thought crossing my mind about this incredible man. As I strode back to my hotel, elated though touched with humility, something crossed my mind that I should have thought of while standing on the Hill of Mars: that first quatrain of Edward Fitzgerald's Rubaiyhat of Omar Kayyam

Awake for Morning in the Bowl of Night
Has Flung the Stone that puts the Stars to Flight
And Lo the Hunter of the East has caught
The Sultan's Turret in a Noose of Light.

I should have declaimed it to the rising sun.

The teachings of Christ and his followers, later called the Nazarenes, were gathered together slowly, painfully and, sometimes, bloodily and taken by Paul, and those who were persuaded by his idiosyncratic interpretations of Christ's teaching in his short Ministry of barely three years, to the Levant, Greece and Rome. After his death around AD61/62 the teachings of Paul, based on his faith in Christ Crucified, the Son of God who rose from the dead after three days, were taken by his proselytes to much of the known world. His Unique Selling Proposition, a term much used in modern marketing, was 'The Love of Christ was open to all, the circumcised and the uncircumcised, regardless of race or religion'. This was his powerful argument and, sometimes, he used it with the skill of a surgical instrument or with the force of a cudgel to convert a pagan away from false gods. Paul, a Jew, failed with the majority of the Jews, but that is a long story.

Over 40 years have passed and, having seen the territory, Paul the man niggled me. He seemed as much a man of our time as of his own. So in AD 2003, having published a Memoir of part of my business life as an international sales-man, I decided to write a book about Paul and his work. But about what? Hundreds, perhaps thousands, of books have been written about him. So I started to read the only source with which I had a passing familiarity, the Acts of the Apos-tles and the Letters of Saint Paul in the New

Testament of the King James version. This totals only 112 pages, half the length of a short novel Not exactly the 3,000 plus pages of Edward Gibbon's Decline and Fall of the Roman Empire. Then the penny dropped. These 112 pages were the sole source of *all* the books written about Paul. The rest was supposition, conjecture, or reference to sources fre-quently dubious and of a much later period. So what was that august bunch of theologians, clerics and historians writing about? Surely not each other's books?

If I were to write about him must I first read Hans Dieter Betz's Der Apostel Paulus und die Sokratische Tradition or E. Lohmeyer's Die Offenbarung des Johannes? I was beaten before I started. In one English book of only 230 pages the attached bibliography was of 152 treatises; and in another, 115. But I *needed* to read some works of others and I was fortunate to have in my own library twenty or so well written works by authors of a questioning disposition. That was what I needed. They were inclined to delve deeply into the 2nd, 3rd and later centuries with many questions to ask.

As I read Acts, etc., questions kept popping into my mind to which I could find no answers. Questions such as: How could Paul not have encountered St. Peter in Rome? How was it that in Jerusalem, a walled city of only one and a half miles by three quarters of a mile in area, could Paul, who had been studying there with the Pharisees for some years, not apparently ever meet Jesus? The priests, parsons and pastors seem strangely unconcerned with such questions.

I wanted the book to be read by laymen, not necessarily devout but who loved the Bible, Old and New Testaments for its beautiful prose and splendid stories. And I hoped to provide an unusual view of Paul the man as well as of Paul the Apostle.

Neither scholar not intellectual, I decided to write as an investigating journalist; posing questions and hoping to find answers. It was like peeling an onion and being surprised at the number of layers, or one of those intriguing Russian dolls which reveal successively smaller dolls as you remove the top one.

Paul may not have been the greatest man that ever lived, but he was surely the most influential and, like Winston Churchill in 1940, his time had come.

2

THE BEGINNING

'I am made all things to all men.'

'I am a man, which am a Jew of Tarsus. A citizen of no mean city.' Thus spoke Saul who was taught the tent makers trade, which stood him in good stead on his vast travels which lay ahead, and from which he could always earn a living. The Roman legions were everywhere, especially in Tarsus, a huge and important garrison town, and soldiers needed well made tents for Winter quarters. To the north and the east it was sheltered by the Taunus mountains, harsh and snow clad in Winter, hot in Summer, on which grazed the herds of cattle and flocks of goats which provided the skins for the tent-makers' craft, the aristocrats of tradesmen. Huge tents housing eight to ten soldiers gave protection from the cold and wet. The wealthy also bought them as useful adjuncts to their houses, and such customers made the makers of the tents quite prosperous. Travellers on the network of Roman roads found them preferable to lice-ridden country hostels; who would not? On his great missionary travels he was always certain of a welcome, food and shelter with fellow tentmakers ; and a thankless task for the proselytising pagans, Jews and others, perfectly happy in their state of re-ligious ignorance, thank you very much.

What kind of city was Tarsus? It lay on the Eastern end of the Mediterranean Sea in the province of Celicia on the River Cydnus and was very old long before Julius Caesar was there in about 60B.C. Saul was probably born 8 to 10 A.D. It was an altogether splendid city, sometimes known as 'Antioch on the Cydnus', and an ancient inscription called it 'The great and wondrous metropolis of Cilicia'. And Strabo, the Greek historian, wrote in 30 B.C. that it had a university to match those of Athens and Alexandria. So, when Saul described himself as 'A citizen of no mean city', he was also saying 'I am a man of a great metropolis, neither rustic nor peasant.' and he was putting down, as it were, a marker, a voice of authority, and you had better listen to it.

Saul's father and grandfather were also tentmakers and well off enough to purchase Roman citizenship. Thus Saul and his siblings, if he had any, could honestly claim the position in society expected by a Roman. Athenodorus, Governor of Tarsus during Saul's father's lifetime, established many reforms, including the right to claim Roman citizenship for 500 drachmae, about two years' wages for a working man. This claim was to give Saul valuable protection from time to time during his journeying. You thought twice before beating a Roman citizen, not that it always saved him from the lash and the stick.

So here was Saul, son of a well-to-do tradesman, a fully paid up member of the middle class, speaking Greek, for that was the lingua franca of the town (Helenised probably at least since the time of Alexander the Great), well educated and a Roman to boot. Before going to Jerusalem as a boy of perhaps 15 or 17, he would have read the Hebrew scriptures, probably the Septuagint, written by 70 Hebrew scholars (hence the name) at the request of Ptolemy Phirodelphus in Greek in the year 250B.C. in Alexandria. And he would, no doubt, have been well versed in the pagan religions, practised and so much a part of everyday life of the city. Tarsus was the supreme example of a busy, bustling

Mediterranean port. Everbody ended up there some time or other, and representatives of just about every nation of the Levant and further afield lived there. No port better earned the soubriquet of 'polyglot', and the principals among these were the Roman soldiers of Eastern origin who were keen worshippers of the Mithraic cult. Mithras, god of light of the ancient Persians and one of their chief deities (the word means ‚friend‘); he is so called because he befriends men in this world and protects them against evil spirits in the next. Sir Thomas Moore in his Utopia called the supreme being Mithras; and the cult of Mithras is thought to have affinities with Christianity. A very tolerant cult it was much loved by soldiers and Saul might have hesitated to dispute it with them, hence his failure ever to return to his birthplace as a missionary. He did return to Tarsus but, as far as is known, only as a private citizen. Never forget he was born a Jew and probably died one, even though he might have had his own ideas about Moses and the Law. The blood aspects of the Mithraic cult he would have found abhorrent, as blood drinking was a fundamental taboo of the Jewish faith.

Mithras was associated with Heracles, a demi-god of Greek mythology, and his slaughtering of the sacred bull. Heracles was ritually burnt every Autumn in a great ceremony which the boy Saul would certainly have seen. A steer would be slain over a pit in which a Mithraic initiate would lie to be bathed in the dripping blood. Rubbing the blood all over his body he would emerge confident he had inherited the bull's power. The duality of worship, Mithras coupled with the death and resurrection in the Spring of Heracles, posed no problems to the Tarsusians celebrating, as it did, life beyond the grave. Central to the myth was the primitive fear of death and the equally primitive hope of immortality. It was a rich and lively belief which attracted the same kind of followers as does spiritualism and similar cults today. It was simple with no room for schismatics and people felt comfortable with it.

The influence of the ancient Hellenic cults, and the even older Persian, was strong in Cilicia, but the people were tolerant of most of them. There was a confident element of harmony as long as one sect was not trying too hard to stuff its beliefs down the throats of others.

For the foot travellers, which included most Tarsusians, Tarsus was fortunate in being at the centre of the finest road network, not to be equalled in Europe until the late eighteenth century; and they were Roman roads. The method was simple, as are most good ideas, depending largely on plentiful local materials, good management, and a supply of labour, willing or unwilling. Kerbstones were set in shallow trenches to identify the road width, and this width was probably standard throughout the Roman empire. Deeper trenches were dug across the width and were filled with stones of graduated sizes, smallest at the bottom to aid drainage and, lastly, large flat stones to form an even surface, casually fitted together like a rough mosaic. The cracks between were filled with pebbles. The result was a flat surface with a long life. And, in the Roman fashion, they were straight. 'The rolling English drunkard made the rolling English roads' wrote G.K.Chesterton. But the Romans were more practical.

An inscription on the tombstone of a Phrygian merchant, in the middle of modern Turkey, proclaims that in his lifetime he made 72 journeys to Rome alone. These sturdy roads, nearly two thousand years old, sped not only traders and armies, but ideas, philosophies and rebellions. They were the forerunners of the railways, airliners, telephone and the internet.

Alas, Tarsus has disappeared with the passing centuries and there is no house on which to place a plaque reading 'St.Paul was born in this house'. There remains but the small Turkish town of Tersoos with a few thousand people and, no doubt, many herds of goats. And of the adventurers who left there over the next Millenium through the Cilician gates to Antioch, to Damascus and to Jerusalem, on four hundred miles of Roman roads, none would stamp his mark so indelibly on history as did Paul.

3

THE END OF THE BEGINNING

'Vengeance is mine; I will repay, saith the Lord.'

'I am verily a man which am a Jew, born in Tarsus, a city in Cilicia, yet brought up in this city at the feet of Gamaliel, and taught according to the perfect manner of the law of the fathers' (Acts 22:3). He said it, according to his devoted admirer Luke, to the gathered crowd in Jerusalem, in Hebrew.

I have written about Tarsus, but what did Saul find in Jerusalem when he reached it, a clever streetwise boy, surely ambitious, though not as a tentmaker? A city probably older than the place of his birth, though much smaller, it was in fact the most glorious, the most magnificent Hellenised city outside of Athens and the creation, largely, of the most reviled man among Christians: Herod the Great (74–4 B.C.). Herod was born an Arab in Idumea in the South part of Palestine, a client King of Rome. He embraced Judaism probably because it was politically useful to do so. The Romans gave him a very free rein, such as they did not grant to his successors. Bearing in mind how tiny was Jerusalem, the size and variation of his architectural masterpieces was astounding.

Within the city walls, an area of one and a half miles at its longest and three quarters of a mile at its widest, there was the Royal Palace and the Temple, itself within a wall some 750 yards by 500 yards. He built the Antonia fortress, prison and Palace, a complex larger and more elegant than the Tower of London, though constructed more than a thousand years earlier, and whose architects and stone masons showed skills at least equal to those of William the Conqueror. An amphitheatre created outside the walls would have excited the Roman crowds with its variety of activities and cruel pursuits, and several aqueducts brought clean water to the townspeople. But the jewel of Herod's architectural creations was surely the Temple on the Mount of Solomon, the successor to the old Temple restored from the ruins of Solomon's destroyed by Nebuchadnezzar after the conquest and removal of the Jews to captivity in Babylon in and around 596 B.C. In its magnificence, its courts and cloisters, there were stones sixty feet long perfectly cut and fitted together, apparently seamlessly, colonnades of marble, fifty feet wide with a circuit of threequarters of a mile and nine gates completely covered with gold and silver.

Jerusalem, at the time of Jesus and Saul, was a city of such architectural wealth and artistic splendour as had perhaps never been seen elsewhere since the world began. Yet it was reduced by a combination of folly and evil to a desert. Nowhere in Rome, in Athens, in Persia, in China or in Europe, where hardly a stone building existed outside of Roman cities, was such magnificence to be observed. But, wherever the armies of Rome marched, in the words of Tacitus, 'they made a desert and called it peace'.

Flavius Josephus (born Yoseph Ben Matatyahu, a Jew) wrote four splendid books, of which the best known are 'Antiquities of the Jews' and 'The Jewish War', subtitled 'Destruction of the Jews A.D.70'. In the latter he describes superlatively the architecture, construction, splendour and beauty of Herod's Palace, the Antonia fortress and,. best of all, the Temple. We know most about him from his own writings but, unlike the Gospel writers, his identity and history are not open to question. With disarming frankness he discourses on life as politician, soldier, orator and historian. A traitor, showing neither shame nor contrition, he served the Romans with unswerving loyalty, finally becoming a rich pensioner of the Emperor Vespasian who, even by the deplorable standards of Rome, practised cruelty of a high order. He became a Roman citizen and changed his name accordingly. Born in A.D. 37 he lived to be sixtythree and so was present in Palestine and Jerusalem during the latter stages of Paul's Evangelism and of his fellows. In fact, he was made Governor of Galilee, at the exceptionally young age of twentynine in A.D. 66. Yet from his writings in 'Antiquities of the Jews', at least in Volume Three of Whiston's edition of 1820 translated from the Greek, he made but one short reference to Jesus and Christianity but to no others. It is worth quoting:

> *'Now there was about this time Jesus, a wise man; if it be lawful to call him a man, for he was a doer of wonderful works; a teacher of such men as receive the truth with pleasure. He drew over to him many of the Jews and many of the Gentiles. He (was) the Christ; and when Pilate, at the suggestion of the Principal men amongst us, had condemned him to the cross, those that Loved him at the first did not forsake him; for he appeared to them alive again the third day, as the divine prophets had foretold, these and ten thousand other wonderful things; and the tribe of Christians, so named from him, are not extinct to this day.'*

This passage is astounding, written by a man whose existence was never questioned and whose dates of birth and death are accurately established.

It was not until the discovery of the first of the Dead Sea scrolls in the spring of 1947 by Mohammed Dib, a Bedouin shepherd, that the world came into possession of a piece of material that dated positively to a time when Christ was alive. The linen cloth in which the Essenes had wrapped the scrolls, written on papyrus, was carbon dated accordingly to the time of Christ. The scrolls must have been older still, and were the complete Book of Isaiah written about 100 B.C.

It has been impossible to establish sensibly the population of Jerusalem during Jesus's ministry. I have seen a figure of one hundred and fifty thousand and that in an area of barely one square mile, much of which was covered by Herod's Palace, the Temple and the Antonia Fortress. Five thousand, I fancy, would be nearer actuality. A figure for A.D. 1622 is given as seven thousand which would probably bear scrutiny. Scholars and historians have always said that population figures, battle casualties and the like from early writers such as Herodotus should not so much be regarded with caution as with downright disbelief. In general they tend to say that what the writer meant was 'there was a great many', on which the scholar put his own interpretation guided by more accurate figures available from the study of later periods. The guess of one hundred and fifty thousand in Herod's Jerusalem was more likely to have been the total population of Palestine, and that at a time of less than twenty million souls in the whole Roman empire. Britain, twelve times the size of Palestine which at that time was eighty per cent desert, could manage perhaps five hundred thousand. An example of numbers exaggeration is that in the first book of Samuel 13:7 in which it is said 'Saul killed his thousands and David his ten thousands, by which Saul was greatly displeased.'

Construction was started in 20 B.C. so Herod was able to

oversee the work before he died in 4 B.C., though it was barely finished before destruction at the end of the Roman Jewish War by the Emperor Titus in 70 A.D. It attracted the Gentile crowds in such vast numbers as to rival visits to Athens to see the Acropolis and Pliny the Elder considered Jerusalem to be a city of remarkable beauty. Whatever tribute Herod rendered to Caesar, his Temple rendered more to the God of the Jews, and from one not born into the faith. The Gentiles came and stood in awe but could not enter beyond its outer courtyards on pain of death. A law which the soldiers of Rome respected even to the point of executing their own who broke the law.

Elsewhere on the Mediterranean coast he constructed the deep water port of Caesarea, a colossal example of military and commercial enterprise. Accompanying this was another palace of such magnificence the Roman governors of the province preferred it to their quarters in Jerusalem and made Caesarea the administrative capital.

His final magnum opus, and the only one to survive the centuries, was Masada, though in ruins. 'A rock with a very large perimeter and lofty all the way along is on every side broken off with deep ravines. Their bottom is out of sight, and from it rises sheer cliffs on which no animal can get a foothold.' Thus began the description of Masada in Josephus' 'Destruction of the Jews'. On this natural rock, two thousand feet above the coast of the Dead Sea, he built a fortress with its own garden for food, silos for grain and huge rock tanks to hold the Winter's rain. He then built a Palace to the same levels of luxury as Jerusalem and Caesarea. The summit was threequarters of a mile round and enclosed within a limestone wall eighteen feet high and twelve feet wide on which he erected thirty seven towers, each seventy five feet high.

At the beginning of the 66 A.D. Rebellion which ended with the destruction of Jerusalem in 70 A.D., a group of Jewish Zealots destroyed the Roman garrison at Masada and held it throughout the War. With Masada as their base they harried the Romans for two years. In 72 A.D. Flavius Silva, the Roman Governor, resolved to crush this outpost of resistance and marched on Masada with his tenth Legion, its auxiliary troops and thousands of prisoners of war carrying supplies across the barren plateau. Silva expected a long siege and that is what he got. At the beginning of the end, that night at the top of Masada. The Zealot's leader, Eleazar Ben Yair, reviewed the options. The Romans would overturn them on the morrow and there was no relief or possibility of escape. It was either surrender or death. They chose death rather than become slaves to their conquerors and nine hundred and sixty men, women and children ended their own lives at their own hands. When the Romans reached the top next morning they were met by silence. The story of Masada was told and recorded by Josephus and the Romans wondered with awe at the resistance and sacrifice of those Jews.

In the Winter of 1975 my wife and I went to Masada from Jerusalem along with a Jewish family from New York on their first visit to Israel. It was cold in Jerusalem which is three thousand feet high but Masada, on the western shore of the Dead Sea was very hot. They had never heard of Masada until they reached Israel. At the fortress as my wife and I climbed to the top they preferred to stay at the bottom and not to go up to see it. I marvelled at this.

To this place came the boy Saul. How old was he? Fourteen? Sixteen? Eighteen? Would a loving father have sent his son away indefinitely at an age less than sixteen? And what did he do when he reached Jerusalem? It has been said, though on the flimsiest of evidence, that a sister already lived there. Did he have letters of introduction, or oral advice that would at least provide him with shelter for a while? If Saul received any such help he never recorded it. Or if he ever told anybody, Luke for example, it was not written down for posterity. He entered into the life of Jerusalem as a blank piece of paper, a palimpsest, on which impressions could be inscribed and then rubbed out as better ideas came forward. He was an innocent on which a beloved teacher could stamp his authority: a void. a vacuum yearning to be filled by priestly lawyers, scholars, philosophers learned in the teachings of the Mosaic Law and the Torah. It was all there in Jerusalem, if you knew where to look. He wanted to be a Jew of Jerusalem, a member of the priestly brotherhood. Going from the synagogue of Tarsus to the Temple at Jerusalem must have been as terrifying to him as it would be to a present day young Catholic seminarist going to serve in the Vatican. It is impossible to know how the boy survived those early years. His trade of tent making and knowledge of tanning and associated businesses would have provided a decent living, but he would have needed much time for study and debate. His father had sent him to study the Talmud and the Torah with the intention, one supposes, of entering the priesthood. That he succeeded in these tasks there is no doubt, nor that he was other than a sublime authority on Judaism and Rabbinic Law.

The Sanhedrin, the guardian authority of the Temple, was a closed circle of Sadducees, priests, administrators, Talmudic lawyers and other members of Jerusalem's great and good; people in the know and people on the make. A modern day comparison would be with the E.U. Commission in Brussels. It was like a club which jealously controlled its membership and Saul must have been clever to have achieved, as it were, associated membership, for he arrived as a young Greek speaking provincial lacking influence or letters of recommendation. A quick student, in no time he would have picked up the vernacular, the Hebrew necessary for his studies and Aramaic, the language of Jesus and the common people.

The titular head of the Sanhedrin was the High Priest, though without a fraction of a Pope's authority. In Saul's day it was probably Caiaphus, he who ordered the arraignment of Jesus before PontiusPilate. Since Palestine had become a province of Rome by conquest, it had become much disliked; particularly during the time of Herod the Great, who ruled harshly and cruelly as a client king of the Empire. On his death the High Priest, appointed anyway by the Governor or even perhaps by the Emperor, was as much a disciplinarian to guarantee freedom from riots and rebellion as he was leader of the Jews. This role was vital as the Governor was swift to punish, sparing not the rod or the cross of cruxifixion. There was a modern parallel in the Russia of the Tsars, where the Patriarch of the Russian Orthodox Church took his orders first from the Tsar, and subsequently from Stalin, rather than from God, and in whose hands the secrecy of the confessional was kept neither in the spirit nor the law.

There is even an English parallel of a sort. William Tyndale was disputing with some lordly divine on the virtue of being able to read the Bible in English, which was a heresy. 'We were better to be without God's law than the Pope's' said the divine. Tyndale replied 'I defy the Pope and all his laws; and if God spares my life ere many years, I will cause the boy that driveth the plough to know more of the Scriptures than thou dost.' Tyndale fled the country in 1524 and never returned. He translated the New Testament by

1526 and the Pentateuch and much more of the Old Testament before he was burnt at the stake at Vilvorde near Brussels on the morning of October 1536.

It is not generally known that there were considerable liturgical and other minor doctrinal differences between the various priestly sects in Jerusalem and, no doubt, throughout Palestine. In no particular order of importance they were:

The SADUCCEES, a smallish group but with great influence, occupied not only most of the important positions in the Temple but also had a majority in the Sanhedrin. Generally they were drawn from the upper classes of Jewish society and strove to avoid change of any sort. They hated trouble, never wishing to anger the Roman governor or his officers. In modern parlance they were reactionary, looking to times past rather than to the future. The Jewish faith was the truth according to Moses, as written firstly on the tablets of stone brought down from Mount Sinai, then written in the five books of the Pentateuch: Genesis, Exodus, Numbers, Leviticus and Deuteronomy. They saw their 'raison d'etre' as keeping the faith within that rigid structure, and the rest of the Old Testament was the history of the Jews on which, perhaps, there was room for discussion or even interpretation. However, the greatest difference between the Sadducees and the Pharisees was that the former did not believe in resurrection and final judgement, and belief in the coming of the Messiah was no more than theoretical.

The PHARISEES feature much more than the other priestly sects in the four Gospels and the Acts of the Apostles; and are vilified, abused and generally hated to an extent that is regarded with suspicion by biblical scholars worldwide. Especially when the words are placed in the mouth of Jesus. For they were well regarded among the Jewish people most of whom, of course, were neither priests, nor scholars, nor other than simple working people. They were mostly teachers and missionaries and were considered to be liberal, not only in a religious sense but in life generally.

Different in may ways from the Sadducees their beliefs were no less profound or less honestly held; they were a large group. There were thought to be about six thousand throughout Palestine and they were frequently employed in quite ordinary jobs and loosely organised. They were more subtle in debate and, to a casual observer, might be compared to the Jesuits from the sixteenth century, though lacking their casuistry and cynicism. It is not for nothing that the Vicar General of the Jesuits is known as the Black Pope. They often interpreted the Laws of Moses differently from the Sadducees which was one reason for friction between them and the packet of rules and regulations put together governing the keeping of the Sabbath, many of them petty, were to the Sadducees verging on heresy. But to the Pharisees these were more relevant to the present day without damaging the profound requirements of the Mosaic Law, one thousand seven hundred and fifty years after Moses brought the tablets down from Mount Sinai. For example, the Ten Commandments instructed the people to keep the Sabbath Day holy. But what did that mean in everyday terms? There was a mass of Pharisaical instructions applicable to just to that single question. And one in particular was absurd. A tailor could not go out carrying his needles late in the day before the beginning of the Sabbath lest they should still be in his pocket when the holy day began. There are many examples in the four Gospels which caused Jesus to call them hypocrites although this was not absolutely fair as most of them obeyed the more seemingly crazy rules themselves. It was the Pharisees who throughout the Diaspora to the various parts of the known world ensured the continuity of the Jewish faith. Few doubt that they were the spiritual ancestors of the rabbinical authors of the Talmud; and it was the great teacher Gamaliel, a Pharisee, who, according to Luke, was broadly on the side of Jesus's disciples. In A.D. 62 when James the brother of Jesus was stoned to death at the behest of the Sadducees it was the Pharisees who lead the protest against the execution and, unlike the Sadducees, they were prepared to argue and disobey the Romans who, under the Governorship of Pontius Pilate, crucified hundreds of them.

Saul was, beyond reasonable doubt, taught by the Pharisees (and possibly by the Sadducees also being '*A Man for All Seasons*' who would have taught him to be a wise man, a debator and a scribe. They certainly did a fine job. His own teachings, therefore, in spreading the Gospel of Christ, who, when Jesus, was the scourge of the Pharisees, is one of the New Testament's major ironies.

The ESSENES, the pure in heart, those who would not compromise, to whom the Law was sacrosanct, unchanging and not subject to argument. They were the kind of people who made you feel uncomfortable; spiritually unclean. If the Jews were indeed the chosen people then they were the chosen of the chosen. In short, they were a theological pain in the neck, and they have their successors in religious intolerance up to the present day.

They seem to date back as supporters of that valiant Jewish fighting family, the Maccabees of about 150 B.C., who successfully resisted the Greek Paganism of Antiochus, a successor to Alexander the Great and ruler of Palestine (175–164 B.C.). But the Romans who came later were another kettle of fish, as history shows. Surprisingly, they were not specifically mentioned in the New Testament.

Frequently they lived in enclosed houses like the future Dominicans and Benedictines, but also among the lay people of whose way of life they fiercely disapproved. Marriage was not encouraged, but grudgingly accepted if only for the survival of the human race. Faithful to God but regarding the Jewish nation as a whole to be unfaithful, only their own leader, the Teacher of Righteousness, could understand the mysteries central to the leadership of Moses. God, they believed, had his predetermined plan which could neither be changed nor enforced by human intervention. They saw everything in apocalyptic terms; when out of chaos would emerge the humble and unquestioning love of God in the Temple.

It remains an enigma why the Essenes were not referred to more over the centuries, from the time of the Cruxifixion until the discovery of the Dead Sea Scrolls in 1948. One must assume that, horrified as they were and suffused with distaste for the decadent, material and wicked world of Jerusalem, as they saw it, they retreated to their closed communities: man's practice throughout history.

The most recent, or at least most dramatic parallel, that comes to mind is the Cathars of the Albigensian Heresy. The Albigensian Crusade, so called, of 1209–71 A.D. was one of the most evil actions of Christianity. In 1199 A.D. Pope Innocent II had declared heresy to be *treason against God*. The target of his wrath was the Cathars of Languedoc. They were spiritual descendents of the ancient Gnostic and Manacheans who saw two faces, those of God on the one hand and of Evil on the other. They believed the prevalence of Evil contradicted the existence of a sole benign Creator. They were vegetarians, ascetic, puritanical and practised a caste of *parfait* (perfect) men and women, and administered the rite of *the laying on of hands*. The movement spread so fast in the remote fastnesses of the mountains between France and Spain (Catalonia) and between Toulouse and Carcassonne, as to have the Pope seething with rage. Something had to be done; the established order was endangered. These Cathars had no time for priests whom they considered corrupt and immoral. Their views on bishops, archbishops, monseigneurs and cardinals, and the vast army of wealthy prelates, positively endangered the whole network of priestly authority carefully put together since Constantine the Great made Christianity the official religion of the Roman Empire. *The rich priest in his palace and the poor man at his gate* suited Rome well. It was the natural order was it not? Worst of all, these Cathars said they did not need priests anyway to intercede on their behalf with God, they could do it better themselves. Christ, surely, would have found no fault in that. Now this was serious. It was like a Trade Union boss being told by the workers he wasn't necessary. The very fabric of society was endangered. The Pope appointed the English noble, Simon de Montfort the Elder, between 1209–1218 A.D.to lead a French army to deal with the Cathars in Toulouse and adjacent towns, and the Holy Inquisition made its presence felt all over the Languedoc. The Cathars had a choice between abjuration or death, and many chose death. In the small fortress town of Monsegur, an important centre of the *parfait,* the leaders of the invading troops asked the Papal Legate, there no doubt to observe that condign punishment was administered, how they could recognise the heretics from the devout. 'Kill them all', he said, 'God will know His own'. Two hundred recalcitrants were burnt alive on a single, massive pyre. This must have given the Church a taste for blood, a flexing of the muscles of the Church Militant and a test run for many and worse massacres of the innocent in the forthcoming centuries.

So, when the Emperor Charles V introduced the papal inquisition into the Empire's provinces in 1521 A.D. and in 1535 A.D. added to it an imperial edict specifying that although unrepenting heretics were to be burnt, *repentent* males were to be executed with the sword and *repentent* females to be buried alive. By the time he had abdicated in 1555 A.D., he and his son, King Philip II of Spain, had, in the Spanish Netherlands, burnt, beheaded, strangled or buried alive some one hundred thousand Flemish and Dutch Netherlanders, Why? Because they were Protestants, and wealthy. The profligate Philip was broke and bankrupt, in need of the possessions of the industrious and thrifty Dutchmen. A sage of the future might have seen in this ideological repression and economic exploitation by the imperial Spanish power an early draft of the history of occupied Europe under Nazi Germany or Eastern Europe under Stalinist Russia.

But to get back to the Cathars; they certainly took some killing and it was not until about 1324 A.D. before they were finally disposed of in the tiny mountain top village of Montaillou. There was no fighting at the end, only a handful of burnings. The members of fifty two families, shepherds, weavers and the like, but including also the Lady of the Manor and the Catholic priest, were examined by the Inquisition headed by Jaques Fournier, who was a local man and, later, Pope Benedict XII. A most meticulous recorder of the most detailed depositions, a virtual history of Montaillou, are to be found in the Vatican library.

In 1998 the Prime Minister of Great Britain (Mr. Blair in one of his acting roles) it was, I think, to do with the belief that peace had been reached in Northern Ireland (it hadn' t), said that he felt the hand of history on his shoulder. Not a bad story to tell if true. In 1981 I sought out Montaillou.

It was still on the mountain top and, though it was May, on the North side of the castle, sheltered from the sun, there was still snow. A handful of people still eked out a living in the village below as they had done for a thousand years or more. I encountered a very old and toothless crone of, perhaps, eighty with whom I carried out a halting conversation since she spoke the almost incomprehensible dialect of the Languedoc. Her family name Clergue, the most diehard of the Montaillau families whose heretical depositions rest in the Vatican and she was a direct descendent. We shook hands and a faint tremor went through me, as I did indeed shake hands with the hand of history.

The ZEALOTS; considering their relatively small number, had a profound effect on the world that over the centuries had followed the horror of the Cruxifixion and spread out in increasing circles, like a stone cast into a pond. They came to represent violent action, opposition to ordered society and struggle against an authority preceived as inimical to their beliefs. The dictionary quotes Zealotry as 'a force aiming to create a Jewish theocracy over the earth." They were more fanatical than the Essenes and more inclined to take the struggle to the enemy face to face; toe to toe if necessary. To them the Romans were a pagan horde whose presence poluted the very air of the Holy Land, and should be driven into the sea.

They held the same beliefs as the Pharisees but their unyielding conviction was that God was the only Master. Six hundred years later a more dangerous and deadly rallying cry was heard; beginning in Medina, which spread eastwards to India, westwards to beyond the shores of Spain and, in less than one hundred years 'Allah al ackbar' 'There is no God but God, and Mohammad is his prophet'. With the Book of the Qur'an in one hand and a sword in the other it was astonishing (or was it) how many of the peoples in the South and Eastern Mediterranian chose the Qur'an. The lean, puritanical men of the Arabian Peninsula were surely the linear descendents of the Zealots, and whose time had come. Now, after a brooding dormancy of several centuries, the Arabic word 'Khilafa', meaning 'a single people of Islam, governed by a theocracy' is beginning to be heard again. Its progeny is lead by such as Osama-bin-Laden, and the foot soldiers are the suicide bombers of Palestine, Iraq, Saudi Arabia and Pakistan. How do you defeat men, and sometimes women, who have no fear of death?

The Zealots seem to have originated in the North of Palestine, the area of Canaan and Galilee known as *bandit country* in the sense that political and religious troublemakers were common there. One of the apostles, Simon the Canaanite, was thought to be a Zealot, also Judas Iscariot, traditionally the betrayer of Jesus. This, on the grounds that his name was derived form Sicarii, a group of professional killers specialising in cutting the throats of Jews believed to be collaborators. If these facts be true, and a caveat should always be in mind, Jesus and, indeed, Saul must have consorted with Zealots and Sicarii. Barabbas (Jesus Barabbas, to give him his full name), pardonned by Pilate at the crowd's behest, who wanted the blood of Jesus, was not a thief but a political activist, a Zealot.

Such people were admired, feared and hated among the townsfolk in equal proportion. Admired because they stood up to and accepted heavy punishment from the Romans; feared because the Romans were inclined to treat both the guilty and the innocent the same when a riot was in progress; and hated because the innocent sometimes were punished as the guilty escaped.

I recall a bitter joke much related in Germany during the

Second World War which sums up the Zealot's nature. The Jews were persecuted in the most cruel manner, and two of them, Isaac and Jacob, were taken out to be shot. The German officer offered, in the hope that it would be accepted, to blindfold them. Jacob silently accepted but Isaac refused and started to bad mouth the Germans in general and the officer in particular. 'There you go again, Issy,' said Jacob, 'Always causing trouble'. That about sums up the Zealots in the time of Jesus.

Jerusalem was an intellectual madhouse, and Saul would have quickly become aware of that. Conflicting sects, all believing in the sanctity and truth of the Pentateuch, yet perpetually engaged in internecine argument on the interpretation of minor points of the Mosaic Law; or the commentaries of renowned, august and rabbinical scholars of the past. Political instability as bad as exists today helped stir the pot of febrile unrest. Though the common folk, those who were, for want of a better word, the *normal* people; Jews by birth and accepting the covenant of circumcision, but unlikely to be prepared to die for Judaism, accepted the presence of the Romans. They were accustomed to occupation and tyranny from outsiders, and settled for the *real politik* of keeping their mouths shut.

If Saul was in a continual state of mental confusion, how could it have been otherwise? The ranting Sadducees believed in free will but not resurrection of the body; that the soul dies with the body, but not in a Day of Judgement, none of which has biblical authority. The Pharisees believed in the resurrection of the body, and the departure of the soul from the body and that some events are predestined and others not. The Essenes believed everything was predestined. To use a modern idiom Saul must frequently have thought his head was done in. In the meantime, it is supposed, he was seated at the feet of Gamaliel the Elder taking it all in, the wisdom, the reflections and, possibly, his best jokes, for, as the world knows, the best jokes are told by the clever Jews.

Is most of this supposition, or is it historical fact? Luke said Saul saw Stephen stoned and in Acts 9:2 he is said to have asked for, and received, letters from the high priest to the synagogue authorities in Damascus, deputing him to arrest and convey to Jerusalem those followers of Jesus who had settled there. There was no information on how he was to do this, and Damascus was more than a hundred miles from Jerusalem.

It is said that Saul might have been a Temple Guard, a typical job of the Sadducees of the lesser sort. That would at least explain the authority given to him to go to Damascus. It also offers the possibility of his being present at the arrest, scourging, trial and Crucifixion of Jesus. But neither he nor Luke, his spin doctor, ever said so. Imagine, in a city only one and a half miles long and three quarters of a mile wide, in which Jesus spent much of his three years' ministry, including two, if not three, celebrations of the Passover, in which he spent much time disputing and arguing with Pharisees and others, and the famous, indeed infamous, incident with the moneychangers in the Temple, Saul apparently never saw or met Him. Is it conceivable that Saul was not privy to any of the dramatic incidents involving Jesus? Moreover, according to Luke (Acts 6:7), many of the Temple's minor officials were already interested in, if not followers of, Jesus, the Jew's unusual *lateral thinking*, as it were, on Judaism.

So what did Saul do during the period b etween arriving in Jerusalem at the age of, say, sixteen in 26 A.D., and 30–33 A.D., the dates at which modern chronologists put the Cruxifixion? We must presume he put in a lot of time studying the Talmud and the Torah, as it is clear from Acts and the Letters (Romans, Corinthians, etc.) he was extraordinarily well versed in the origins and history of the Jews, and extremely devout. The nature of Jerusalem gives valuable clues. If, at that time in history, these were cities with centres of manufacturing and primitive industries, using iron, copper and clay, making dyes and textiles (everybody needs clothes) they did not include Jerusalem. It was a place of relative poverty and short on comfortable living except for the wealthy. That also suggests a small population and a hill town on inhospitable and unfertile slopes. Jerusalem remained a poor city almost to the present day, certainly until after the Second World War, one thousand nine hundred and fifty years later. What it did have, though, was the Temple and Herod's Palace and these were money spinners; plus the many annual religious festivals to which Jewish pilgrims came from all over the Diaspora. They came from Thrace, Macedonia, Athens, Corinth, Asia Minor, Pisidia, Antioch, Tarsus, Cappodocia, Cilicia and many other places.

At the Festival of Pesach alone it is said that twenty thousand sheep were butchered in the Temple for sacrifice and these would have fed on the scrubby poorly pastured hills outside the town. These would have provided markets, horse and cattle markets and a host of what are called service industries. Plenty of sheep, goat and camel skins formed a lively leather business. And if you had the skills of a tent-maker with a religious bent, Saul could not have chosen a better town. He had all the competence for earning a decent living. In the Letters he is proud of being self sufficient, and in Luke's account of Paul's trial in Jerusalem he admits to being prosperous. He would probably have been sought out by pilgrims from his own town of Tarsus. So, putting all this together, an educated and employed young man may well have been a notable amongst trades people, the bourgeoisie, and the lower echelons of the Temple. Certainly he would have taken on board lock, stock and barrel all the Mosaic Law's proscriptions, such as those concerning dietary affairs, eating with Gentiles, and rigid obedience to the Sabbath. He was a Jew (though of the Diaspora) through and through. As he said in Phillipians, 'Circumcised the eighth day, I was born of the race of the stock of Israel, of the tribe of Benjamin, an Hebrew of the Hebrews, as touching the Law of Pharisee.'

He was as packaged as a young twentieth century politician on the climb up the greasy pole of promotion, in those few years of Jesus's ministry. He would have kept all those covenants which to a non-Jew seemed irritating and petty, but which bonded the family and the race together; the glue which ensured the unbreakable strength of a people across two thousand years of pogroms, massacres, humiliations and mass expulsions *before* Hitler's 'Final Solution' leading to the Holocaust.

Despite this packaging, and the determination, not of the apostate, but of one set on success, he could not entirely escape the influence of his early life in Tarsus where, although a Jew, the Hellenistic way of life was strong. Greek philosophy of many schools and the Mystery Religions were studied and discussed openly and he was no stranger to the poetry of Epimenides, Aratus and Menander. He must also have taken in some of the liberal teachings of Gamiliel, who saw Gentiles as a challenge, ripe for proselitisation, and which later influenced his decision to make Christians out of Gentiles, leaving the Jews to Peter and his brethren.

So now we have it, Saul in Jerusalem for at least seven years with few facts sbout that period verifiable. Almost everything I have written so far is supposition, conjecture or traditional thinking, and we know how accurate that can be. Then like two locomotives colliding, or a Spanish bull leaping the barrier to gore the terrified audience, or the villain bursting onto the theatre stage, Saul appears for the first time in Acts 7. They say Irishmen are not born, they emerge fully grown, roaring drunk, from the primeval slime. Well Saul, not drunk but fully grown, certainly burst onto the Biblical scene. When I was a small boy of ten, bullied and humiliated by bigger boys of twelve, a normal procedure in growing up, I was not allowed to play in a game of football, but allowed to guard the other boys' coats, but with guile always managed to wriggle into the game. The first thing Saul does is to volunteer to guard the coats of those fanatical Sadducees or others stoning the blasphemous Stephen. Do you think he could have resisted *not* joining in and throwing rocks at poor, innocent Hellenised, non-Jewish Stephen, the first Christian martyr? I don't.

4

O DEATH WHERE IS THY STING, O GRAVE WHERE IS THY VICTORY?

'The last enemy that shall be destroyed is death'

At this point it might be useful to write down a chronology of events:

	A.D.
Pentecost	30–33
Events down to Paul's Apocalypse	before 40
Paul's Apocalypse	late 30
Paul's first two missionary journeys	44–49
Paul's stay at Corinth and return to Antioch	49/50–51/52
Paul's third missionary journey	after 51/52 before 57/58
Paul's arrest in Jerusalem and hearing before Felix	57 or 58
Paul's custody at Caesaria	59 or 60
Paul's appearances before Festus	60
Paul's two years in Rome	60/61 or 61/62
Acts of the Apostles, possibly written by Luke, possibly not	60/62 or 61/62
Gospel of Saint Mark possibly written in Rome	about 70
Gospel of St. Matthew possibly written in Antioch based on Saint Mark	85
Gospel of Saint Luke possibly written in Corinth based on Saint Mark	80

The Epistles of Saint Paul were almost certainly written before Acts. It follows, therefore, that with the Epistles written before the Acts, and Acts not written *before* 62 A.D., and with Mark the source of the Synoptic Gospels not before 70 A.D., Paul was then dead, or at least disappeared. Thus any knowledge Paul had about the ministry of Jesus could only have come from oral contact with Jesus himself or his Apostles, on which there is no evidence either way.

The only thing certain about the New Testament is that though scholars and theologians have studied and deconstructed the evidence and commentaries over the centuries, they have never managed to establish beyond reasonable doubt when, where and by whom the Gospels were written. There was the oral tradition of Jesus, written down by the writer of Mark, which provided the material for the writers of Matthew and Luke, who then altered and added to suit their own audiences. John, because it was so different in style to the other three, collectively known as the Synoptic Gospels, is the most mystifying. John lacks the ethical content, the homely structure of the Synoptics; is more theological. A significant difference is that it contains no mention of Jesus' birth or early life. In that, of course, John is similar to Mark. One must not lose sight of the fact that the Gospel authors were not historians as would be understood in a modern world.

After witnessing the stoning of Stephen, Saul may have had doubts on the wisdom of such an odious crime. There is no evidence, of course, but as a student of Gamaliel (Luke in Acts 22:3 puts into Saul's mouth 'I was brought up in this city at the feet of Gamaliel') who clearly had liberal and open minded leanings, though a Pharisee of high degree and a doctor of law, he must have observed his teacher in action. When the Apostles were hauled before the Sanhedrin (Acts

5:34) Gamaliel defended them, privily addressed it, quoting an historical event to support his defence 'And now I say unto you, refrain from these men and let them alone. For if this counsel or this work be of men it will come to nought. But if it be of God ye cannot overthrow it; lest haply ye be found even to fight against God.' I fancy that already the seeds of contradiction in his character, which are evident in many of his Epistles, became apparent after Stephen's death and before the event on the road to Damascus.

Now we have Saul on the horns of a dilema. What influenced him most; in what direction was he drawn? The dogmatic teachings of the Sadducees; the liberal, jesuitical inclinations of the Pharisees; the unyielding austerities of the Essenes; perhaps the harsh, even murderous, attitudes of the Zealots? Not to mention the strict discipline required of a temple guard. It was the latter that seemed to prevail. Now he was to start on the *awesome* journey from Jerusalem to Damascus, and thus to his death in Rome. Whatever his subconscious thoughts about the death of Stephen, he must have been in a turmoil, a towering rage to do what we are told he did. What *did* he know about him? Well, he must have known he was one of the seven Greeks appointed to do the menial work, waiting at table, etc., while the Apostles went about the business of proselytising and praying, spreading the teaching of Christ. In return for which Greek widows received some financial support. It follows from this that Saul must have hated the pressure being put on his fellow Jews to move away from the strict observance of the Law. He was, after all, a Jew with no doubts about Judaism, its history and its future as the chosen of God.

It must have been in that frame of mind he went to the High Priest and applied for letters to the synagogue of Damascus authorising him to arrest men and women following the New Way and to bring them to Jerusalem. The authority of the High Priest and the Sanhedrin must, at best, have been suspect or, at worst, spurious outside of Jerusalem, or even Palestine. So what powers could they have had in Damascus? That there was a large Jewish settlement in the Gentile city of Damascus, a part of the Roman province of Syria since 65 B.C. is indicated by the number massacred there at the outbreak of the Jewish revolt in 66 A.D. (according to Josephus). Some of them had fled Jerusalem, influenced by the teachings of the Apostles, fearing reprisals from the Sanhedrin; even though considering themselves to be good Jews. It would have been among the majority, Sadducees, Pharisees, or anyway Jews without taint of heresy in the Sanhedrin, to whom Saul would have looked for support in removing those in Damascus considered heretical.

How these arrests were to be made and how those arrested were to be secured, fed and watered is not made clear. Nor what forces Saul had at his disposal to ensure that the, one supposes, unwilling captives covered the one hundred miles or more to Jerusalem without loss, is not touched upon. Perhaps the momentous happening that was to befall him made the original purpose of the Damascus journey so irrelevant that further details became unnecessary. This was just as well as it might have taken a military operation using many armed men to transport a body of unwilling men, women *and* children on the journey. A costly operation; and who would have paid for it?

There is an historical footnote about the death of Stephen. Was he a Greek from outside Jerusalem, or was he a Greek speaking Jew from the Diaspora, resident in Jerusalem? He was not a Christian, because at that time no such existed. He can be considered a martyr but not of the Christian faith; there wasn't one. At best he must be considered an acolyte or follower of the Apostles and they, whatever their change in attitude towards Judaism, were Jews. As was Jesus; as was Peter; as was James the brother of Jesus; and as was Saul, who died a Jew also, it is believed.

When Stephen was brought before the council and asked to explain himself, he responded by declaiming a potted history of Judaism from Abraham to the present day, directly from the Pentateuch, while professing his undying beliefs as a good Jew. Though he said they had always killed the prophets, as they killed Jesus. Had he lived and listened to the views of Saul there would have been many arguments, and an agreement to disagree. His death is often referred to as a 'lynching' and not an official stoning; as the priests said to Pilate 'It is not lawful for us to put anyone to death'. (John 18:31). Had it been official, the execution would have been done in accordance with the instructions in the Mishnah, that centuries old collection of Oral Law, in which the condemned felon was thrown from a great height and, if he survived, or she survived, was despatched with a single huge stone. So it is impossible to know the precise circumstances in which Stephen met his death.

Paul, now with his papers of authority to present to the Damascus synagogues, departed. Though before departure, according to Acts 8:13 he put in some practice, making havoc of the dwellings used by the new acolytes of the Apostles. 'Entering into every house and committing men and women to prison.' Shortly before Damascus, how close is not explained, nor who was with him, 'He fell to the earth when a light shone around him, hearing a voice say to him 'Saul, Saul, why persecutest thou me?' Saul said 'Who art thou Lord?' and the Lord said, 'I am Jesus whom thou persecutest; it is hard for thee to kick against the pricks,' This is how the Apocalyse of Saul is described in Acts 9:3–5. Those sixteen words of the Apocalypse which changed the life of Saul are of immeasurable importance; for without them there would have been no Christianity. Exceeding in impact the words of Jesus when he said to Peter 'You are the rock on which I will build my church.' If there is a modern equivalent of equal apocalyptic impact, it may be that statement of Otto von Bismarck, Chancellor of Germany in the 1850's, when he said 'The most important fact of the 19th century is that the United States of America speak English.

Yet at the moment of this frightening Apocalypse Saul had but scant knowledge of Jesus of Nazareth or, if he had, no knowledge of His crucifixion and resurrection. It defeats logic, but not by a single word does Luke suggest that Saul, his friend, had any prior knowledge of Jesus. Friendship is implied when Luke writes in Acts, using the first person 'We', that he was with Saul in Philippi.

The story of Saul's Conversion is told no fewer than five times; three times in Acts, once in Corinthians II (11:32–3) and once in Galatians I (1:12–17) and, broadly speaking, they are the same. Though in Corinthians and Galatians Saul mentions neither the Damascus Road, the blinding light nor a voice from Heaven. Though this does not mean they did not occur. Another difference in the accounts of Saul is that he is at pains to make; it clear that his revelation is unique, personal and direct from Christ Resurrected; owing nothing to the testimonies of Peter, James or John. In Galatians I (12–17) Saul says:

For I never received it of man, neither was I taught it, but by the revelation of Jesus Christ. For ye have heard of my conversation in times past in the Jew's religion, how that beyond measure I persecuted the church of God, and wasted it. And profited in the Jew's religion above many of my equals in mine own nation, being more exceedingly zealous of the traditions of my fathers. But when it pleased God, who separated me from my mother's womb, and called me by his grace, to reveal his son in me, that I might preach him among the heathen; immediately I conferred not with flesh and blood. Neither went I up to Jerusalem with them which were Apostles before me, but went into Arabia and returned again to Damascus.

There it is, without equivocation. Saul saw himself as Christ's personal envoy, with the task of converting the non believer, with no need even to consult with the disciples of Jesus. The side-tracking of the Nazarenes had started; by the end of the first century A.D. they had lost out to the Paulites.

But I digress; after the Apocalypse, according to the Acts, Saul, struck blind, was led to Damascus and remained so for three days until one Ananias restored his sight, and said he had been sent by Christ to tell him 'He is the chosen vessel unto me, to bear my name before the Gentiles, and Kings, and the children of Israel.' The voice of Luke in Acts says nothing of Saul's statement in Galatians, even though the chronologists are certain that the Epistles were written years before Acts. Acts merely says that Saul's spiritual encounter made him welcome in Damascus by those he had come to persecute. And it was the Jews of the synagogue who tried to murder him.

So, after the dramatic escape in a basket over the city wall, he disappeared, he says, to Arabia. To do what? And for how long? He does not say. By Arabia he probably meant the territory of the Nabateans, east of the River Jordan, the area of ancient Petra and prsent day kingdom of Jordan. Could it have been a retreat to do some serious thinking before returning to Damascus (as he says he did) after a short while where he remained for three years.

At that time Saul must have thrown, metaphorically, his cap into the ring. He now knew what to do. He had already decided that his vision of the risen Christ, the Messiah of whom Isaiah and Ezekiel prophesied, was on his way and he was the apostle chosen to lead the vanguard. To save the Jews from themselves; to cleanse Judaism, to convert the Gentiles to the worship of the Jewish God through his son Christ; without the baggage of circumcision, dietary laws and the mishmash of petty rules. The Nazarenes, the followers of Jesus, might still look to Jesus as a Messiah who would deliver the people out of the hands of the Romans. But Saul's Christ was not the anointed warrior king, but a leader that would conquer by grace and love and faith in Heaven; not in this world but the next.

To the apostles the death of Jesus was a calamity. To Saul it was a triumph. Life, the true life, began with the death of Jesus on the cross and the risen Christ. Saul has a vision of God unequalled in its ruthlessness until perhaps Martin Luther who was doing no more than following in the footsteps of Saul. Though Luther, a man of his time and therefore an anti-semitic, might have had some difficulty in accepting Saul as a Jew.

5

PAUL MEETS PETER

'Be ye angry and sin not;
let not the sun go down on your wrath.'

There were three meetings only: the first was about three years after the events in Damascus, in Jerusalem. Though in Acts 9 Peter is not mentioned by name. In Galatians *Saul* says he met him. The second was fourteen years later in Jerusalem. And the third was some time later in Antioch, where Saul was many times.

Not much you may think for the last apostle to meet the first; whom Jesus appointed with the words 'Come ye after me , and I will make you to become a fisher of men.'

The first visit. according to Saul, lasted fifteen days; the second was a short visit only and the third in Antioch, at which time he upbraided Peter for hypocrisy. If the first meeting was in, say, 36A.D. about three years after a possible crucifixion date; and the second fourteen years later in 50A.D.; and the third in Antioch about two years later in 52A.D. they met only three times in sixteen years and never thereafter.

The Apostle Jesus trusted above all others and with whom He had eaten many times; embraced many times; whose mother-in-law He cured of a fever; the Apostle whose feet, along with the feet of the other eleven, were washed by Him; the Apostle who had seen the nail holes in Jesus' hands and feet and the wound made by the Roman soldier's lance in His body; Saul met but briefly and over a long time, he who knew none of this. Can we believe this? We must believe it though it strains credulity. Have the great and the good who study these things never put them up for discussion? Have they never passionately debated at Canterbury or Rome, Catholic seminaries and Protestant Colleges of Theology? It was as though Stanley, having searched the jungle for Livingstone in 1871 and finding him, said 'Doctor Livingstone, I presume', turned on his heels and went back to America. This surely is the most ignored and least considered story of the New Testament.

- Peter was with Jesus throughout the three years of his ministry.
- He was with Him at the three Passover suppers.
- He was with Him in the Garden of Gethsemane when he was arrested.
- He was with Him during the scourging; during the trial before Pilate.
- He was probably with Him at the crucifixion.

Yet Saul apparently knew none of this. He was thirty years in and around Jerusalem and neighbouring provinces during his three missionary journeys yet there were *so* many things about Jesus that he did not know. Or, at any rate, they are not mentioned in Acts or in his Epistles. It is worth recording a few of these:

- Jesus in the wilderness and the temptations by the Devil.
- Jesus throwing the moneychangers out of the Temple.
- The parable of the sower and the seed.
- The parable of the prodigal son.

- The parable of the ten virgins.
- The parable of the good Samaritan.
- Jesus saying to Peter 'You are the rock on which I will build my church.'
- Jesus saying to Peter three times 'Do you love me?' to which Peter replied three times, 'You know I do.' To which Jesus replied three times, 'Feed my sheep.'

These were all stories which must have been common currency in Jerusalem and Galilee and they illustrated the nature of people; their strengths and weaknesses; their cruelties and kindnesses; their wisdom and foolishness. It was such tales that identified Jesus in the eyes of the common people as no ordinary mortal. As for the miracles, news of those would have spread like a forest fire, and the poor would have had no difficulty in believing He was indeed the Son of God, although only on one occasion did He admit as much (John 10:35–37). Saul would have been no stranger to miracles and magic stories in his native Tarsus. They were the stuff of Greek and other's gods and demi-gods. Truth, history and legend were not separated in the minds of the people, poor or rich, and Saul would have believed them, along with everybody else.

None of this does Saul, after his apocalypse, ever report to those Gentiles and Jews whom he urged to believe in Christ, who offered them grace and love. It was almost as though he deliberately discarded as unimportant anything that happened before the Crucifixion and Resurrection . One might think that to tell the story of the woman at the well in Samaria, (John 4:7–26), the good shepherd (John 4:1–16), and the Transfiguration of Jesus of the mountain in the presence of Peter, James and his brother John, would have strengthened his own belief in the Resurrection.

Of all the omissions, I find the absence of any reference to the Sermon on the Mount as described in Matthew (Chapters 5–7) the most remarkable and puzzling. This very long sermon, said to have been heard by thousands from all over Galilee, Jerusalem, and beyond the river Jordan, is virtually the complete canon of Jesus' teaching and in its Authorised Version cadences, construction and poesy is unequalled in its advocacy of how people should believe and act towards each other. Of all the teachings, mystical or ethical, in the New Testament, it is what most Christians, devout or occasional, know something about. Not even the Lord's Prayer (the only time it gets a biblical mention is in the Sermon) receives a nod of recognition from Saul. Even though it is Jesus' instructions on how to pray to the Father. Could it be said that for Saul these were two men, the mortal Jesus, who taught the moral and ethical Law, and Christ who, at the moment of death and then Resurrection, became Christ the Son of God and the Holy Ghost; Christ of the Apocalypse who spoke to him, appointing him his apostle of the New Way to purify Judaism and make it the universal faith embracing the whole of mankind? Did Saul think that Jesus prepared the way for Christ of the Cross, as John the Baptist prepared the way for Jesus? How else can it explain his reluctance, or failure, to propagate the teachings of Jesus of Nazareth the Jew, as Saul was a Jew?

So now this man, this very modern man, appointed directly by God through His son, Christ, as His sole Apostle to carry to the known world, outside the narrow confines of Israel (Palestine), the Word of the New Way: accept of the love of Christ, pray to Him for the forgiveness of sins, and on death your soul will go to Heaven to be with God the Father. For he said in his First Epistle to the Corinthians:

'But if there be no resurrection of the dead, then is Christ not risen. And if Christ be not risen, then is our preaching vain, and your Faith is also vain.'

Thus armed, certain in his beliefs, confident in his ability to complete the task given to him alone, brooking no argument (for how can the truth be arguable?), he made his way to Jerusalem. A little late, perhaps, but there was no hurry; his was an act of courtesy and not absolutely necessary. But what did they talk about, Peter the simple fisherman, unlettered but not unwise, accustomed to hard knocks in defense of his beloved Saviour; and Saul, the educated, sophisticated, Greek speaking Jew of the Diaspora, and student of Gamaliel the Pharisee?

Now we must enter somewhat into the realms of fantasy, and I make no apology for drawing loosely on the Monty Python film 'Life of Brian'. For what ensued during the meeting must surely have been reminiscent of what passed for dialogue in that film:

Somewhere in Jerusalem, Peter is with James the brother of Jesus, when there bursts in on them this small, balding, bandy legged, staring eyed and hook nosed bloke. 'Hello, Pete', he says, 'I'm Saul. It's a long time ago, more than three years in fact, but you must remember me, I was the one who egged on the crowd that was stoning Stephen. Should have kept his mouth shut, of course. He was a Greek and on a hiding to nothing. You don't remember me? Well, in those days who would. I was a general dogsbody in the Temple, did a bit of policing for the Sadducees, and I'm really sorry about Stephen. Anyway, I was thirsting to go off after some of your mates who'd legged it to Damascus to bring them back to the High Priest who was pretty upset at their stepping out of line – asking awkward questions and not bothering too much about what they ate. But not to worry, nothing came of that and I'll tell you for why.' At that point Peter thinks he is having a visit from the devil and is tongue tied. But this cove carries on babbling. 'Somewhere near Damascus I had this vision thing. I was chucked to the ground and a blinding light shone on me, and a voice from the sky said 'Saul, why are you always getting at me, causing trouble?' Trembling all over, I asked 'Who are you?' and the voice said 'I'm Jesus whom you are bad mouthing, and I'm fed up with it and I'm going to make it hard for you if you don't pack it in.' Anyway the light went out and I couldn't see, and the others led me into Damascus, and I was blind for three days. Then a bloke called Ananias came. Said he had been sent by God to give me my sight back and to tell me that God had chosen me to go in his name to convert the Gentiles, and Kings, and the Jews to a proper way of thinking, and I was to become his top Apostle. '

'I suppose he thought with my foreign lingo skills and being a good organiser, Sanhedrin trained and that, and used to the tricks of the Pharisees, and (lets face it) modern and experienced in foreign travel, he reckoned you and your mates were a bit limited in outlook. O.K. when dealing with the peasants in Galilee, Capernaum and the other places, but out of your depth among the smart arses of Antioch and Ephesus, not to mention Athens. He thought you'd done a good job so far but now we're in another league and playing for higher stakes. We're going after the kings and the Romans, big stuff.'

Peter now has a blinding headache but this maniac goes on and on: 'Anyway, no reason why we can't be good friends. Jesus would like that. And there's plenty of local work to do, try the Samaritans, but take my advice and stay away from Jerusalem, they are a very nasty lot here and too friendly with the Romans, especially that toe rag Pilate. Well, I've got to get on, the work of Christ is calling. Ta ta for now and, by the way, I'm going to change my name to Paul, Saul sounds so Jewish, don't you think?'

Peter, poor Peter, was ready for tears. He and his mates had given up everything for Jesus; lived with Him, shared everything, been tested by Him many times, had seen the nail holes in His hands and feet, risked their lives for him, been beaten in the riots and Jesus had even washed their feet. He must have looked at James the brother of Jesus and perhaps said in his rough Galilean dialect 'Heyup, Jim, we've got a right one here. What are we gonna do? A new boss has been appointed and I've been made redundant by that snotty nosed little chancer.'

Well, who knows, I *could* have written 'Full and frank discussions were held' as the politicians would say.

6

PAUL MEETS PETER AGAIN

'For where no law is, there is no transgression.'

A lot had happened since the first meeting. Peter's activities are to be found all through Acts which were written many years after the Pauline Epistles. Of unknown authorship, but usually considered to be by Luke who certainly considered himself to be a friend of Paul, and may even have met him, Acts maintains a pro-Roman and anti-Jewish bias throughout.

One happening which had outstanding relevance to the second and third meetings between the pair was the vision Peter had on the rooftop in Joppa. He was hungry, but fell asleep while awaiting the preparation of food. In the vision he saw a huge sheet caught up at the corners descending from Heaven to the ground. In it he saw 'All manner of four footed beasts of the earth and wild beasts, and creeping things and fowls of the air.' Then a voice came to him, saying, 'Rise Peter, kill and eat.' But Peter said 'Not so Lord, for I have never eaten anything that is common or unclean.' To which God replied, 'What God hath cleansed, *that* call not thou common?'

Now this recounting of such an astounding experience may well have been a powerful piece of propaganda on the part of the author of Acts in support of Paul's disdain for the Jewish dietary laws, which he used to persuade Jews away from Judaism and towards Christ. In parallel with this, and also contigious with it, was the meeting with Cornelius.

Cornelius was a Roman centurion in the Italian Cohort of Caesarea. A cohort was a part of a legion, about six hundred men in a legion of six thousand. It was important that the cohort in which Cornelius was a centurion, commanding about one hundred men, was the 'Italian' in which all soldiers were Roman citizens and *not* auxiliary soldiers recruited locally. Cornelius had a dream in which an angel of God told him to send for Peter; who duly went to Caesarea, and with Cornelius 'vouchsafed' of God, baptised him. Peter's own vision, which gave him freedom to eat what previously had been unclean to him, also allowed him to associate with a non-Jew whom he, ante-vision, would have been forced to consider ritually unclean. So now, with one bound as it were, Peter had become free of the Jewish dietary laws and had baptised a Roman citizen. The value of these two events seen together are incalculable. Jesus' first Apostle, born a Jew, associates with an unclean Gentile and baptises him to receive the Holy Spirit of Christ crucified. And who is it he baptises? A Roman. Yet there is no evidence that Paul ever knew about these. Yet what could he have made of them among the Jews in Antioch, and the seven churches of Asia: Laodicia, Ephesus, Smyrna, Sardis, Pergamum, Philadelphia and Thyatira. Of course, since these stories occur nowhere else other than in Acts, it is not surprising Paul does not speak about them as he was almost certainly dead when Acts were written.

Meanwhile, Paul was labouring in many parts of Syria and Cilicia; also in Athens. There he met with such formidable opposition that he never returned. Antioch in Galatia, Antioch in Syria, Ephesus and Lystra among others saw him many times, but not Athens. The Athens visited by Paul circa

50 A.D. was quite different from the populous, prosperous and politically powerful city-state of the fifth century B.C. Nevertheless it was still highly regarded and retained its position as the philosophy study centre of the world. It was generally known as the Academy; hence the expression 'Groves of Academe', Paul was rather unlucky to arrive in Athens during a resurgence of Platonic philosophy, a most sceptical discipline, which had been in the doldrums for several hundred years. Central to Plato's philosophy was personal morality, the law, politics and righteousness which were all of a whole. This was anathema to Paul who could not stand the Athenian's contempt for the Christian dogma. He was met first with silence, then ridicule, as they scoffed at the Resurrection story. He was accompanied by Timothy whom he sent back to Macedonia. Possibly to protect himself from the Athenian sceptics, Paul preached in the market places and in the synagogues, with little effect. Even his powerful sermon delivered from the Hill of Mars, the Areopagus, seems to have fallen on stony ground. Hundreds of years of philosophical study and debate, and a city full of smart alecks, defeated Paul. Had he known more of Jesus' ministry he would have taken on board the wisdom that proselytisation is most likely to succeed among the poor and humble than the rich and proud. Frankly, Paul was out of his depth in Athens.

Now, according to Galatians, he went up to Jerusalem for the second meeting with Peter, which he said he was instructed to do by 'revelation', taking Barnabas and Titus with him. The fact that Titus, a Greek, was uncircumcised suggests he was a convert but not a Jew. This did not seem to trouble the Jews he met. They knew by then he was having success in converting Gentiles to receiving the Holy Spirit of Christ, who were, of course, uncircumcised. The Jews met, were friends, edging towards conversion, while continuing to believe devoutly in circumcision *and* the dietary laws. He met James the brother of Jesus, John and Peter (whom he correctly called Cephus), and it seems that the Nazarenes, led by Peter, recognised they had reached a parting of the ways; an avoidable division of labour, and that Paul should look to the conversion of the Gentiles (the uncircumcised) and Peter to the Jews.

In the words of Galatians 2:7–9, Paul speaking:

'When they saw the gospel of the uncircumcised was committed unto me, as the gospel of the circumcision was unto Peter. For he that wrought effectually in Peter to the apostleship of the circumcision, the same was mighty in me toward the Gentiles. And when James and Cephus and John who seemed to be pillars, perceived the grace that was given unto me, they gave to me and Barnabas, the right hands of fellowship; that we should go unto the heathen, and they unto the circumcision.'

This second, and crucial, meeting is sometimes called the Apostolic Council of Jerusalem.

Now we have it. Paul, born a Jew, seeing that the future of Christianity (as it was later to be called in Antioch) lay in the abandonment of most that was sacred to the Jews since the circumcision of Abraham two thousand years before; triumphing over Peter, the first apostle appointed by Jesus the Jew of Nazareth, and Peter apparently accepting gracefully? I wonder. The irony would not have escaped Peter, on reflecting, as reported in Matthew 10:5–6:

'These twelve, Jesus sent forth, and commanded them, saying, Go not intothe way of the Gentiles, and into the cities of the

Samaritans enter ye not, but go rather to the lost sheep of Israel.'

History is written by the victors.

Then began the corraling, the sidetracking, of the Nazarenes, who ended up finally as a small sect of Jewish Christians based in Jerusalem. Before Paul strode on to the scene they represented the mainstream Christian view; and their leader was James the brother of Jesus, Joses, Simon and Judas; sons of Mary the wife of Joseph. We are told they thought Jesus neither divine nor born of a virgin; but a great prophet, a devout Jew and the Messiah.

After the fall of Jerusalem in 70A.D. the Nazarenes, whose importance was already greatly diminished, retired to the small town of Pella, beyond Jordan. Their first Bishop was Marcus, and under him they renounced the Mosaic Law. They spread towards Damascus and became the despised Ebionites. They were regarded, as were the Primitive Baptists by the Church of England in the nineteenth century and much of the twentieth, as being below the salt, the church of the lower orders. Acts 15 reports a debate with Paul about whether Gentiles can be admitted to the Church. They blamed the Gentile Church (i.e. Paul) for distorting the message of Jesus and directly blamed Paul for this. Ultimately, the Ebionites were rejected by the Jews as apostates, and the Gentiles as heretics. It never profits one to be first with a good idea; and the revolution always devours its own.

Paul and his followers went on their way and Peter, with some of his brethren, on theirs. Each had their devoted companions with unswerving belief in their leaders. Both sides distrusting the other; both united in the love and grace of Christ. Though it is remarkable how few of Paul's friends seem to have knowledge of Peter's friends. Look at these two lists and observe if any of the names on the left are to be found also on the right. And, remember, Jerusalem was a small town.

PETER	PAUL
Andrew	John, son of Zebedee
James and John, sons of Zebedee	Mark
Philip	Timothy
Bartholemew	Lydia
Thomas	Aquila
Matthew	Priscilla
James, son of Alpheus	Erastus
Thaddeus	Aristarchus
Simon the Canaanite	Tichicus
Simon the Leper	Agabus
Barabbas	Ananias
Simon of Cyrene, the Cross Bearer	Simeon Niger?
Mary Magdalene	Drusilla
Mary, Mother of Christ	Festus
Joseph of Aramathea	Rufus
Cornelius the Centurion	Titus
Mary and Martha of Bethany	Luke
Lazarus, brother of Mary and Martha	Felix
Nathaniel	
Nicodemus	
Barnabas	Barnabas
Gamaliel	Gamaliel
Stephen	Stephen
Tabitha	Ananias (Damascus)
Barsabus	Barsabus
Silas	Silas

These lists are not long, but indicate with devastating clarity that there was little or no commingling between the rival camps of Paul and Peter. The absence of Jesus' Apostles, save John, son of Zebedee, is quite puzzling. I would suggest that Paul's forthright views on the irrelevance of circumcision was a good enough reason for the friends of Peter to keep their distance from the friends of Paul.

I have referred several times to Paul's apparent ignorance of the happenings during Jesus' short ministry of three years. Perhaps this was deliberate, so as not to be influenced by anything which pre-dated the Crucifixion and Ressurrection of Christ. It could also be because he had never met the Apostles, save for Peter and John son of Zebedee, in whom, anyway, he showed scant interest.

7

PAUL MEETS PETER AGAIN,
BUT NEVER AGAIN

'If the trumpet gives an uncertain sound,
who will prepare himself for the battle?'

The third and last meeting is described in Paul's Epistle
to the Galatians; written from Rome. How it got to the
brethren in Galatia is unknown as no courier is named.
Galatia was a large tract of present day Turkey, extending
from Ankara (a town built in the 1920's by Kemal At-
taturk as a new capital to replace Istanbul, which he
hated), to the southern coast area which included Cyprus,
about fifty miles offshore. At the time of the Epistle there
were several communities whose conversions from Gentiles to faith in Christ Paul had started during his first two
missionary journeys. They were gathered together loosely,
in what were called 'churches' for want of a more accurate word, at Lystra, Iconium, Derbe and Pisidian Antioch
(not to be confused with Syrian Antioch). Antioch in
Syria was a very old town built by the Romans in 300
B.C., exceeded in size only by Rome and Alexandria.
Antioch and Jerusalem were where the most dramatic
episodes of Christian proselytising took place. They were
frequently at loggerheads with each other in the manner
of Florence and Sienna in the fifteenth century, but
without the bloodshed. Jews of the Diaspora were well established in their synagogues, as were the Greeks, and

present in large numbers. It was a Graeco-Roman city and a veritable polyglot of peoples.

Paul's habit in a fresh territory was firstly to contact the synagogue, the natural thing for a Jew to do. Then, based on the military concept that time spent on reconnaisance is seldom wasted, he was able to find out who was important, who had influence, who was friendly or unfriendly. Thus he was able to save time, and for a man as impatient as Paul certainly was, that was important. Clearly he made great penetration among the Hellenes, if not within the synagogue, and in due course Antioch became the city where the word 'Christian' was first used.

He based his teaching on a very simple proposition. All you needed to do to receive the love, protection and blessing of God was to have faith in His Son, Christ. Nothing could have been simpler, and a people yearning to believe in something flocked to a preacher who promised, indeed guaranteed, a splendid afterlife in Heaven. Such a proposition was attractive to rich or poor, educated or illiterate, and easily understood. And when he said in Galatians 3:28 'There is neither Jew nor Greek, there is neither male nor female, there is neither slavery nor freedom; for ye are all one in Christ Jesus.' that would have endeared him to the poor, if not to the authorities.

There is an uncomfortable parallel with the Islamic religion, in which the powerful slogan 'There is no God but God, and Muhammad is his prophet' was such a rallying cry to the Arabic people, who were fellow Semites, that Islam spread through the Middle East like a forest fire. From 630 A.D. the third religion derived from the Old Testament sped on its way and the descendants of Ishmael, the son of Abraham by Hagar, Sarah's bondswoman, were set on revenge for the wrong done to Hagar and Ishmael when

Abraham cast them out into the wilderness after Sarah delivered Isaac. With Muhammad claiming direct descent from Ishmael and thus from the loins of Abraham, would Paul from his secure place among the saints have been surprised at the emergence of Muhammad and Islam?

Little is said about Pauline successes in the synagogues of Antioch or the other cities. It was among the Hellenists, the Greek worshippers of the old pagan gods since the days of Homer and the Greek philosophers, who found his teachings most powerful. All went well until the Jewish converts, followers of Jesus and faithful to His teachings in every way, came from Jerusalem and, like him, they had few doubts about the sacredness of the Mosaic Law, especially the covenant of circumcision, the dietary laws and marriage, none of which Jesus ever spoke against during the three years of his ministry.

Paul now found himself in an unenviable position. He had brought many Hellenists over to his persuasive evangelism, only to find his exhausting efforts being attacked and undone by these Nazarene Jews who were troubled that he, a Jew, now considered the very core of the Mosaic Law, circumcision and diet, to be irrelevent, and was teaching the converted pagans that faith and nothing else. He brought them to Christ and they should not be constrained by those items of the Law, The Nazarenes, on the other hand, said they could not come to Christ uncircumcised. There were rows and bitter arguments but Paul knew what had to be done and he was not one to compromise. The act of circumcision was *too* great an obstacle for grown men to accept. He believed, with the greater conviction, that he had by revelation been appointed by Christ himself to be the Apostle to the uncircumcision as was Peter to the circumcision, to which, however reluctantly, Peter agreed during the second meeting in Jerusalem.

These old and sacred Jewish practices, held since the times of Abraham and Moses, would not and could not be forsaken by the Nazarenes. Though accepting that Paul held the same faith as did they, many broke contact with him. This was a mighty struggle and there could only be one winner. Paul had to establish clear blue water between his simple new teaching, and the complicated web of archaic Jewish practices, which were neither of theological nor spiritual value, and would keep the Jewish religion confined to Palestine. One important casualty was Barnabas, Paul's great friend, a young Jew born in Cyprus, and who had accompanied Paul to Cyprus on the first missionary journey, also on the second. He broke with Paul for the same reasons as the Nazarenes.

Well now, what mattered more was that Peter was already in Antioch before the Nazarenes arrived and Paul found him eating with Gentiles. Nothing wrong with that, of course, as far as Paul was concerned, he welcomed it. But when the Nazarene Jews came from Jerusalem Peter withdrew from the Gentiles in fear of what James the brother of Jesus would say when he heard about it.

There was an almighty row with Paul who accused him of hypocrisy and wrote the following in the epistle to the Galatians 2:11 onwards:

'But when Peter was come to Antioch, I withstood him to his face, because he was to be blamed. For before that certain came from James, he did eat with the Gentiles: but when they were come he withdrew, and separated himself, fearing them that were of the circumcision.'

That was the third meeting between Peter and Paul.

Then in the Epistle for the benefit of the Greek converts, Paul explains why he was in such a rage with Peter and the other Nazarenes, and he describes the second meeting with Peter in Jerusalem. Paul was accompanied by Barnabas and Titus. Galatians 2: 7–9:

> 'But contrariwise when they saw that the gospel of the uncircumcision was committed unto me, as the gospel of circumcision was unto Peter; (For he that wrought effectually in Peter to the apostleship of the circumcision, the same was mighty in me towards the Gentiles:) And when James, Peter and John who seemed to be pillars, perceived the grace that was given unto me, they gave to me and Barnabas the right hands of fellowship, that we should go unto the heathen, and they unto the circumcision.'

This was indeed the crossing of the Rubicon for Paul, and as far as is known they never met again. Nor, for that matter, is there any mention of meetings with any other of the Apostles. The chronology is such that when Paul was back in Jerusalem, arrested and imprisoned, then taken to Caesarea, he never met Peter.

Paul, after his meeting, probably came to a view about Peter; that he did not have the strength of character to break absolutely with the strong ties of Judaism. After all, why should he have done so? His life with Christ had never suggested he should be other than a true and faithful believer in the God of the Jews, of his fathers. Was not Jesus a Jew, the Son of God? Then there was the Apocalypse on the road to Damascus. Did it happen? Or did Paul have a mental lapse and imagine it? Peter would have been less than human if a doubt or two had not crossed his mind.

The Bible is full of coincidences and parallels. The departure of Barnabas is strangely similar to John 6:53–66 in which Jesus tries to explain the meaning hidden in the eating of His flesh and the drinking of His blood. Some of his followers were horrified and, in verse 66:

'From that time many of His disciples went back and walked no more with Him.'

It could be said that from this point began Paul's historic struggle, *not* with the forces of paganism and idolotry but with those who should have been his brothers in Christ, indeed *were* his brothers in Christ. This might be said to be the first of the many schisms that were to split and splinter the Christian Church for many centuries. But Paul had triumphed, he had created a new Church which, though hardly bigger than a pebble when he died, became a mountain by the sixth century A.D.

8

THE APOCALYPSE
AND THEN WHAT?

'My strength is made perfect in weakness.'

There is a surprising gap of fourteen to seventeen years between Saul's Conversion, to the first of his three missionary journeys; and virtually nothing is known of his activities during that period. While in Damascus, subdued, even humble perhaps in the presence of those he had come to arrest and take to Jerusalem, he must have felt that something positively elemental had changed his character. He was not the man who left Jerusalem, breathing fire and brimstone in pursuit of heretics and blasphemers. Certainly whatever had happened to him on that Damascus road, vision, dream, apoplectic fit or confrontation with Christ, he would never, ever be the same again. 'Converted' is the wrong word. Converted to what? Not to a Christian, the word was not to be used for another thirty years. 'Apocalypse' must do. A strange happening, he thought, had caused the spirit of Christ to enter into his soul. He was not like one of Jesus' Apostles who had wandered with Him through the villages and hills of Palestine. He had stepped sideways. The Crucifixion and the Risen Christ had become part of him. He did not feel superior to Peter and his brethren, but he felt different. He was different from them, with a different mission. They had been followers of Jesus and he was sure he was the spiritual companion of Christ the Son of God, given a specific duty: to clarify, to simplify the link that must be forged between Gentile and Jew,man and woman, slave and master, with Christ.

Paul was an urban man, a townsman. The Apostles were easy going rustics who saw things simply through the parables, miracles, healings and exorcisms of Jesus. They were not looking for reasons or explanations, wanting only the comfort the very presence of Jesus gave to them. Paul was a troublemaker, a thorn in the flesh of authority. To be thus in the Damascus of those times was fraught with danger. Where he saw opposition to his arguments he attacked it head on, bull at a gate, that was his way. He was not one to offer the soft answer that turneth away wrath.

There was chaos, not short of civil war, in Damascus and the troublemaker was the Ethnarch, Aretas. His daughter, divorced by Herod Antipas, who had beheaded John the Baptist in order to marry Herodias, his niece and sister-in-law, fled to her father's court in Petra, capital of Nabatea. Aretas, outraged by this treatment of his daughter, bided his time, then invaded Antipas' territory in Northern Syria, routed the Jewish army in his path and established himself in Damascus. Now this did not go down at all well with the Emperor Tiberius (who was Herod Antipas's mentor when he was fooling around in Rome), and he ordered Vitellius the Roman Prefect in Syria to deliver Aretas to Rome, dead or alive, lest his action be considered an insult to Roman authority.

So the town, in a state of revolt, was no place for a man of Saul's temperament. It is also said that his preaching irritated Aretas; which is why he quit Damascus, traditionally it is said, in a basket lowered over the walls at night. He left that place of anarchy torn apart by religious and political conflict. The very condition Saul wanted to alter by a process of synthesis through Faith in the living Christ.

The screen then goes black, as it were, he disappeared. In his own words, he went into Arabia (Galatians 1:17), which must have been the land of the Nabateans, South of Damascus, into what is today the Kingdom of Jordan. Possibly into the sizeable towns of Philadelphia (modern Amman) and Petra. Wherever Saul went he would not have been idle. Perhaps he may have entered into a lonely retreat for a period while he pondered on the enormous, frightening tasks that lay ahead. But to do nothing? No, that was not Saul's way. Perhaps he was putting together his 'Gospel', planning how he could deliver it, packaged, to people who, if he was lucky, would love him for it; or, if not, chase him out of town. This did indeed become his lot. He was flogged five times (for some reason the number of strokes given is put at 39 for each flogging). Further, he was imprisoned three times and shipwrecked three times.

During this three year absence, probably towards the end of it, he made his way to Damascus by way of Jerusalem. Here he met Peter for the first time. How they never met during the years they were both there must have puzzled the scholars and theologians over the centuries, though I have never read it nor heard it discussed in my lifetime. The meeting lasted fifteen days, after which he is said to have gone to Tarsus, the town of his birth, by way of Syrian Antioch. Although the only evidence for this is the few words of Luke in Acts 9:30. Paul never said he ever returned to Tarsus, but he went somewhere out of the way. Perhaps to such towns as Derbe, Lystra or Iconium. There were plenty of places in which to dissolve into the crowd if he so wished. But how did he live, a stranger in new places? This would have posed no problem if he retained his skills as a tentmaker, a good living was to be had in any place that needed tents, which was just about everywhere in Asia Minor.

If he did, as he normally did, provoke authority, particularly in the synagogues, and landed up in prison, a report would have filtered back to Damascus or Jerusalem. We know nothing and it remained thus for some ten years.

Meanwhile, as Paul was pondering on his future, there were developments in Jerusalem very disquieting to the Jewish conservatives, especially in the Sanhedrin. There Jesus' followers, and other influenced by the teachings of Jesus, were drawn from among the younger priests and their friends, and this was a Temple based, singularly Jewish phenomenon. The older priests were shocked. The elevation of the man Jesus to the Messiah, the Son of God, was blasphemy, striking at the monotheistic worship of God himself.

It is likely the stoning of Stephen set off alarm bells among those dissidents, Jesus' followers, Gentiles and Greek speaking Jews, and they might have become persuaded that Jerusalem was becoming too dangerous for their own safety. Hence many moved to Antioch, a reassuring threehundredandfifty miles distant from Temple influence. Others moved to the largely Gentile city of Caesarea, parts of Samaria, to Alexandria and other towns in North Africa.

So, long before Paul began his lonely task of preacher, teacher and evangelist, many of whom were to become the seedcorn for him, were already preaching the cult of Jesus in distant places. Paradoxically, that was to make his work harder. Although in Paul's view they were generally going in the right direction, their personal compass was a bit wonky, causing deviation from the Way, and needed Paul's teachings, based firmly on the Crucifixion and triumph of the risen Christ, to get them back on course. For a fresh start all the dogma, dietary laws and the irrelevance of circumcision needed to be abandoned.

Antioch was a very fine city, sophisticated in the manner

of Athens; a big trading centre with a vast aquaduct, which was much admired by lesser towns, bringing fresh water fifty miles from the South East. There were public baths, stadia for various pursuits, theatres and plentiful evidence of the elegant gods of the Greek mythology; statues and wall reliefs of Apollo, the Minotaur and Theseus were to be seen. Its ambience was comfortable to the Hellenes and there was no shortage of synagogues for the dissident young Jews. It was better, of course, for the Gentile followers of Jesus to be in with but small danger of persecution. In Jerusalem the Jewish escapees would probably have only eaten kosher meat from the Temple, but in Antioch they would have had to buy in the markets, without knowing or caring whether the meat was kosher or killed in a pagan temple.

There came a point in time when Paul shook the dust of Jerusalem from his feet, so to speak, and migrated to Antioch which, in a casual way, was the starting point for his journeying. For a very long time it became the accepted centre for the teaching of the New Way and in the future was linked always strongly with Paul and then Saint Paul, He was not totally finished with Jerusalem, far from it, as in about 57 A.D., against all advice, he went there by way of Tyre and Caesarea and finally, after imprisonment and several trials, by ship to Rome.

So in Antioch, Paul the Hellenised Jew, then the Jerusalem Jew, then the post Apocalyptic Apostle of Christ to the Gentiles, places himself there to organise his ministry to all those throughout Asia Minor whom he could buttonhole, cajole, threaten or convince to give up paganism, or strict observance of the Mosaic Law and worship the Risen Christ, and come to God through faith alone. That was his task for the next twenty years.

9

PAUL'S FIRST
MISSIONARY JOURNEY

'I am debtor; both to the Greeks and the Barbarians;
both to the wise and the unwise.'

This takes place after Saul/Paul's return from Jerusalem to
Antioch after the meeting with Peter, James the brother of
Jesus and John the son of Zebedee; no other Apostle is mentioned. According to Acts 13:1 the Holy Ghost spoke to the
converted in Antioch saying 'Separate me Barnabus and
Paul for the work whereunto I have called them.' Now
Barnabus, a Jew from Cyprus who was living in Jerusalem,
is first mentioned in Acts 4:36 when he lays all his goods at
the Apostles' feet to go into the common fund.

So they set sail for Cyprus, taking the young John Mark
with them as an assistant, in today's jargon as a ,gofer', a
dogsbody I suppose. Why Cyprus? Well a start had to made
somewhere and Barnabus must have known his way around
the island. Barnabus would have known the Apostles well.
His real name was the Jewish Joseph, who might have put
himself up for election to the Twelve to replace Judas Iscariot. Some traditions identify him with Barsabbas who lost
out to Matthias in the election; another of the Apostles
never, ever, heard of again. He was thus already a Jesus follower when he met Paul, not yet influenced by him.

They left from Seleucia in Pieria, near the mouth of the
Orontes, the first of many sea voyages to be made by Paul.

He said he was *shipwrecked* three times. Sea travel was remarkably easy and in the Mediterranean reached an intensity in the first and second centuries not to be equalled until the fourteenth century.

One must not forget that much of Acts, as written by Luke, was propaganda. He wanted the two routes of the Way; that of the Jesus followers, the Nazarenes, Jews through and through who wanted change without compromising their belief in the Pentateuch and the Torah ; and the new teachings of Paul, to be compatible. He clearly favoured Paul over the Jesus followers but must have known that serious theological conflict was inevitable. But amity reigned when they went to Cyprus and Barnabus would have been in ignorance of Paul's game plan: his cards were very close to his chest, the time not yet ripe to declare his hand. Luke was suggesting, or at least implying, that the early Church was always Christian, whereas the word was no more than a nickname for a Jewish sect.

They landed at Salamis, an ancient Greek port nearest to Seleucia and, as had become Paul's practice, went to the nearest synagogue. He was, as it were, 'using the facilities' – very clever. The question of his name change seems never to have been reflected on but, on Cyprus, Luke changed it to 'Paul' over 'Saul' because it was Roman, a race with whom he could find no fault. If *Paul* was a Roman citizen in Tarsus, and there is acceptable evidence that he was, then he could claim a Roman name, or rather three names, which was the privilege of Roman status. If it was Paulus, his full name could have been Gaius Julius Paulus. Paul means 'small', and to fit into a basket which lowered him down the walls of Damascus he *must* have been small. From now on we shall call him Paul. Nothing is recorded in Salamis of his activities. One can only surmise he was politely received, but did not get any interesting vibrations, and so left for Paphos in the South West of the island, a large city containing many Greeks, and probably well known to Barnabus.

Under Roman rule Paphos was big enough to be called a metropolis, which didn't mean much except it was, from time to time, the Governor's seat, and the Governor's name was Sergius Paulus. In his entourage was one Bar Jesus, a Jewish sorcerer posing as a prophet. He is represented as being a magus, a religious sorcerer, and his closeness with the Governor suggests Sergius Paulus had some interest in religion. How the Governer came to meet Paul is never explained but, clearly, he was a willing listener. Bar Jesus, sensing hostile competition, did his best to ridicule Paul's teaching, but unsuccessfully. Paul countered by blasting him in a speech composed almost entirely of phrases taken from the Septuagint's 'Son of the Devil' and, it was said, struck Bar Jesus blind. The outcome was that the Governor became a believer, so Paul had a Roman scalp to dangle from his belt, that of a Governor no less. But he did not baptise him. Why not? Peter had baptised Cornelius the centurion in Caesarea. I suppose one Roman officer must have been worth at least one hundred civilians.

Nothing else is known about Paul on Cyprus, though it was thronged with Jewish and Gentile communities. With Sergius Paulus as his friend and patron one would have thought an extended visit might have given him many conversions to the Faith from both Jews and Gentiles. I doubt if he was working to a strict timetable. This is another of those lacunae missing parts, in the life of Paul, which is so very aggravating.

Leaving Paphos they went to Perga in Pamphylia on the South coast, North of Cyprus. Its current name is Antalya and John Mark decided to leave them. No explanation is made, no reason given. Perhaps, having observed Paul's modus operandi, he said 'Thanks, but no thanks', and returned to Jerusalem. Now this was a very serious matter. Barnabus was discomforted and wanted John Mark to stay. But with Paul you were either with him or against him; no compromise, no prisoners. He did not try to persuade John Mark to stay. This should have been discussed in depth by Luke in Acts but it is not. At the end of the mission, back in Antioch, Barnabus broke with Paul, never to travel with him again. The break must *surely* have been on the move away from certain fundamentals required by the Mosaic Law, determined by Paul.

They continued their journey as far as Pisidian Antioch, a difficult journey through arid mountains, in territory peopled by tribes of uncertain temper, regarded as dangerous and capricious in attitude, known to prey on travellers. Paul was aware of such dangers and he wrote about them in Corinthians 2 11:26:

'In journeying often, in perils of waters, in perils of robbers, in perils by mine own countrymen, in perils by the heathen, in perils in the city, in perils in the wilderness, in perils in the sea, in perils among false brethren; In weariness and painfulness, in watchings often, in hunger and thirst, in fastings often, in cold and nakedness.'

Pisidian Antioch was the site of the most important of the Roman colonies founded in the area by the Emperor Augustus. In his inimitable way Paul found the synagogue and he, along with Barnabus, was received civilly. After the reading of the Law and the Torah Paul was invited to address the congregation which he did, at length. First the potted history, from the escape from Egypt onwards. This was his first substantial speech recorded in Acts and is intended, perhaps, to be the model of his approach to preaching to Jews and, as in Athens, his speech represents how he dealt with a Gentile audience. The coming of Jesus as Messiah is described as the culmination of God's dealings with the Jews, His promise delivered. The Jews' rejection of Jesus is seen as due to ignorance rather than wickedness; and the Romans, as usual in Acts, were exonerated from blame. Paul then tells of the appearance of the risen Christ, seen by many witnesses, as further evidence of God's promise to the Jews. The speech finishes with the promise of the forgiveness of sins to those who believe, and a threat to those who do not.

Not a man to mince his words, Paul. *Tact?* That was for the weak and mealy mouthed. He was no seeker after popularity and had a skin like a rhinocerus. He seemed to welcome the kicks and thrashings that came his way from hosts that rightfully felt insulted and aggrieved. But on this occasion he seems to have been fortunate. The 'God fearers', like the centurion Cornelius, usually Gentiles who attended the synagogue and adopted certain Jewish practices but not circumcision, accepted him and, no doubt, a few were converted. There was no riot, a certain amount of pushing and shoving perhaps, caused, according to Luke in Acts, by the Jews out of 'jealous resentment' But the synagogue and town authorities were not anxious that Paul should stay, so they left Pisidian Antioch while they were winning, over the mountains to nearby Iconium. This was another Roman settlement with many Greeks, other Gentiles, but not many Jews, though there was a synagogue. He must have wondered at the inconsistancy and capricious nature of his fellow men, for in this place, full of Gentiles, full of pagans, the corn should have been ready for the sickle, the fruit awaiting harvest. He was puzzled. If the population was awaiting a messenger from the Gods it was not him. There was no immediate hostility, he was listened to and might even have had the effect he wanted from a few who accepted the message. Then the trouble started, it is said by 'unconverted Jews'. The word unconverted is used to remind us that at the time not all Jews were hostile, and some were becoming believers. Perhaps there were some attracted to the Way as taught by the Apostles, and had fled Jerusalem, as other young Jews had fled to Syrian Antioch. Like many others later, having heard Paul in full throat, ridiculing circumcision and the dietary laws, they were not best pleased, and joined the Greeks in yet another stoning of Paul and Barnabus. Comparatively unharmed they escaped to the Lycaonian cities of Lystra and Derbe, no great distance.

These were small towns, somewhat primitive, and undoubtedly full of pagans. How on earth Paul made himself understood in such places is a mystery. They spoke neither Greek, Latin nor Aramaic, and a sophisticate like Paul must have felt uneasy to say the least, wasting his time. Anyway, he had not planned to be there and it was just a place of refuge from Iconium. Then there was an incident of pure farce. In Lystra Paul heals a lame man and the people, observing this magic, this sorcery, shouted in their native Lycaonian lingo 'The Gods have come down to us in human form.' Paul did not understand, of course, at least not straight away, but when he saw the preparation for a pagan sacrifice (the people thought he was Zeus, and Barnabus, Hermes) he was thunderstruck, jumping up and down in a rage. Clothes rending is mentioned in Acts 14:14. The Greek Gods were clearly the people's choice. He did, however, deliver a very clever speech (did they understand it?), saying that 'God sends you rain from Heaven, and crops in their

Season, and gives you good cheer in plenty.' Now this is what ordinary pagans wanted to hear from their God, a speech for Gentiles, rather than for Jews or 'God fearers'.

But they were by no means safe in Lystra, as a posse of Jews arrived from Antioch and Iconium to inflict chastisement and this caused a change of mood among the Gentiles, and they were stoned out.

Nevertheless, when matters settled down, as they do, they returned briefly to Iconium and Antioch to establish some sort of ad hoc churches to encourage the converts. It is impossible to know whether the converts numbered in the hundreds or were counted in dozens – probably the latter. There is no information and anything said by Luke on the question of numbers is inflated by his desire to paint Paul's endeavours in a good light, and why not?

This first journey was nearing completion and Paul, with Barnabus, returned to his base in Syrian Antioch, *not* by the more direct overland route from Derbe to Syria through the Cilician Gates and Tarsus, but by sea from Perga where they had landed from Cyprus, direct to Antioch. This would have taken much longer. Why was the shorter, quicker land route not taken? Again, there is no information. Could it have been to avoid going to his town of birth, Tarsus, where he must have had *some* family? How strange and, surely, out of character. Perhaps he had heard that aphorism of Jesus: 'No man is a prophet in his own country.'

10

PAUL'S SECOND
MISSIONARY JOURNEY

'The love of Christ which passeth knowledge.'

Paul took Barnabus and Titus with him for the second meeting with Peter, James the brother of Jesus, and others, in Jerusalem. The fact that Titus was an uncircumcised Greek was not without significance, since his presence, indeed his right to be there, was accepted by Peter and the other Jesus followers- all Jews, all circumcised, all adherents to the dietary laws. There was an uneasy peace, and the division of labour broadly agreed upon: Peter to the Jews, Paul to the Gentiles. Peter's followers, however, while agreeing, perhaps grudgingly, that Gentile converts need not undergo circumcision (Paul used the words 'foreskin' and 'circumcision' as labels for Gentiles and Jews, Galatians 2:7), they were adamant on the dietary laws and demanded:

'That ye abstain from meat offered to idols and from blood and from things strangled.'

Before the end of this meeting there was a caveat. Certain Pharisees, who had converted, believed that no Gentile's conversion could be complete in his acceptance of Christ Crucified without circumcision and the practise of the dietary laws. That was the Mosaic Law and it was obligatory. It was not surprising to find lawyers, Pharisees and members of Judaism devoted to the strictest interpretation of the Law. What *was* surprising was that they were prepared to sacrifice the beliefs of their many generations of forefathers to place their unquestioning faith in Christ. Their's was the greatest sacrifice of all. To his credit, Peter (Acts 15:7–11) spoke against this Pharisee view, but whether he was acting as a peacekeeper, or really *did* disagree with the Pharisees is anybody's guess. A compromise was reached, (itself a great rarity among Jews), and when Paul and his party left to return to Antioch they were accompanied by two of the Jerusalem community, Judas and Silas, bearing a letter to be read to the Antioch Gentile converts and others. In effect they were sent as 'minders' to ensure that Paul told the correct tale to his Antioch brethren.

As to Paul, he considered circumcision not worth an argument; in his view it was an irrelevance. Women, after all, were not circumcised. As to the dietary laws, he certainly did not intend to force them onto his converts. But he remained silent on these matters while in Jerusalem. It must be said, though, when he wrote to the Galatians from Rome about the third meeting with Peter in Antioch, his story is somewhat different. Beyond the comprehension, perhaps, of most at the Jerusalem meeting, only Paul could understand the inevitability of the schism, the break, that was to come between the uncircumcised, diet disobeying Gentiles and the Jesus followers of Peter, converted Jews. He *knew* the time had not yet arrived to speak openly about it. It was as though an omelette had been jointly prepared only for the Jesus followers to decide it was uneatable and for them to try to unscramble it back into the egg shell impossible.

Barnabus, however, seemed to be able to read between the lines. He was troubled when Paul quarrelled with John Mark at the departure from Cyprus. For the second missionary journey Barnabus wanted John Mark to be with them, but Paul wasn't having it. Barnabus, upset, wouldn't go without him and, along with John Mark, returned to Cyprus. Unusually for Acts, as Luke always gave the impression of sweetness and light between Paul and his companions, there is a record of this argument in Acts 15:37–39. The dissension, first started by the quarrel about John Mark, was almost certainly theological in origin rather than being a case of imcompatibility.

Paul takes Silas with him, whom he first met in Jerusalem, and they returned to Antioch together. Possibly he chose Silas because he was a Roman citizen (he also had the Roman name of Silvanus and was *not* a Jewish convert like Barnabus and John Mark, who had become suspicious of Paul's evangelising style; a Jew when with Jews; a Roman when with Romans; and both when with other Gentiles. He had begun to show increasing antipathy to the Mosaic Law.

They headed in the general direction of Galatia using, no doubt, the straight, well paved Roman roads; by way of Tarsus (when once again he does not seem to have stopped off to see family and friends), Derbe, Lystra and Iconium. In Derbe, or perhaps Lystra, it is not clear, he meets up with Timotheus (Timothy), son of a Greek father and a Jewish mother. He was a convert, a Gentile, and not circumcised. There is no information on how they met but Paul wanted him with him. And what Paul wanted, Paul got. Moreover, and this stretches belief, he persuades Timothy to undergo the painful and rough surgery of circumcision .

'Him would Paul have to go forth with him; and took and circumcised him because of the Jews which were in those quarters; for they knew all that his father was a Greek.' (Acts 16:3)

What a salesman! Paul could have sold snake oil nostrums to the early American settlers; or refrigerators to the Esquimos. But what a hypocrite, if true. Acts describes it as historically authentic, and it has always been fiercely attacked because of its inconsistency with his principles expressed in the Epistles.

I had a dear friend of many years, whose early childhood in the 1920's was spent in Turkey where his father was an electrical engineer. He often spoke of seeing young Turkish men and boys, walking about holding their long gowns away from the body. It amused and puzzled him until his father, somewhat embarrassed, told him they had just been circumcised, and were holding their gowns away from a very sore place. Poor Timothy, such obedience.

Paul's first task was to visit and consolidate the work he had done during the first journey with Barnabus in the towns of Derbe, Lystra, Iconium and, of course, Pisidic Antioch. No trouble was reported, bearing in mind the riots and stonings of the first visits. They made known to the converts the decisions and pastoral responsibilities agreed upon in Jerusalem with the Apostles and elders of the Jesus followers.

Thereafter it had been Paul's plan to travel West from Iconium and Antioch to what was loosely called Asia; visiting such cities as Ephesus, Pergamon and Laodicia. But, apparently, he is delivered of a message from the Holy Spirit *not* to go to Asia. We are not told how the message was delivered. Then he considered pushing across the border at Mysia between Asia and Galatia, possibly to Nicea and Nicomedia, but another message came from the Holy Spirit forbidding this also. These messages are taken as evidence that Paul is being Spiritually guided in the direction of Europe, away from Jewry. There is yet a third vision or Spiritual message in which he sees a Macedonian begging him to go over to Macedonia; and that is what he chooses to do.

So they make for the coast of Troas by way of the heavily wooded and mountainous Western route, and took ship to the island of Samothrace; and the next day to Neapolis. With adverse winds it could have taken five to six days. Because of poor navigational knowledge, with neither compass nor astrolabe, vessels of the period hugged the coastline whenever possible. For, when out of sight of land, hardly a seaman knew West from East. This condition remained more or less until that unlettered but clever Yorkshireman, John Harrison, in the middle of the eighteenth century designed a clock of such accuracy that it varied in time less than one second over a twentyfour hour period. Thus could longitude be accurately measured, and the Greenwich Meridian established. The scholarly astronomers and mathematicians were not best pleased with the success of this working class fellow and tried hard over many years to deprive him of his just reward. Macedonia is a huge area extending from the Northern end of the Aegean to the Adriatic, and was a Roman Province.

The first port of call was Phillipi, founded by Philip of Macedon, father of Alexander, a Roman colony since 42 B.C. This second journey was by far the longest of the three and, with the first, which was principally to Cyprus, may have taken five years, covering as it did from Syrian Antioch to Troas and then on toPhillipi, Thessalonica, Athens, Corinth, across the Aegean to Ephesus and finally by sea to Caesarea in Palestine and then North to the starting point of Antioch, his home, if Paul could be said to have had a home.

Unusually, on reaching Phillipi, Paul did not seek out the

synagogue; there seemed to be few Jews. He had a fortunate encounter with the woman Lydia, a seller of purple fabric and Acts says 'a believer in God', meaning, one supposes, a Gentile 'God fearer' who had been taught or influenced by the Nazarenes. She was from Thyatira and she and her family were baptised by Paul and, in consequence, are regarded as the first to be baptised in Europe. Lydia might even have *been* a Jew but, in any case, she did not seem to be concerned with dietary laws or circumcision. It is a fact that women were more receptive to his teachings and, despite his reputation for misogyny, he frequently gave women considerable authority. Lydia was just one of many. She was wealthy, and Paul was mostly short of money. By contrast there is no evidence that the Jerusalem church of Peter ever gave authority to the women converts.

Paul, not without reason, considered himself badly treated at Phillipi. There was the occasion when he removed an evil spirit from the fortune telling slave girl; as a result of which her masters had Paul and Silas flogged yet again, and imprisoned. An earthquake broke down the prison walls and Paul could have walked away free but he did not. He had the gaoler eating out of his hand for not running away. Paul refused to leave until the magistrates themselves came to the prison to release them having, as Paul lectured them, committed a grave offence in jailing two Romans. This is, of course, a story by Luke in Acts which we accept or we do not. But it is a *good* story and Paul can be said to have had some modest success. Lystra was a great distance from Rome and it was curious, as well as fortuitous, that Paul found a woman convert like Lydia there. It begs the question of how many converts were already in Rome, a good fifteen hundred miles from Jerusalem, and they would have been Jesus followers too. It would be another ten years before Paul was in Rome. His stay in Phillipi was brief and he never went back.

Thessalonika was a few miles West and, on arrival, he found, as usual, the synagogue. There was a large Jewish community, rock solid in their opposition to Paul's rhetoric, and after a space of three Sabbaths he admitted defeat and left. Why should he have bothered with the circumcised? Yet again he was breaking the Jerusalem agreement with Peter and James.

Acts deals with Thessalonika in a mere nine verses (Chapter 17). Luke's version of the visit is quite different to Paul's in the Thessalonian Epistle. For example, Acts says he was in the synagogue three times. Paul never mentions this, and hardly mentions the Jews at all. Certainly he does not say, as Acts 17:5:

'But the Jews who believed not, moved with envy, took unto them certain lewd fellows of the baser sort, and gathered a company, and set all the city in an uproar.'

Who should we believe, Luke or Paul? Luke never lost an opportunity to blame the Jews for any trouble which befell Paul. Again, according to the Thessalonian Epistle,

Paul, Silas and Timothy stayed much longer than two weeks (three Sabbaths) and gained Gentile converts *not* Jewish.

He also left them with the impression (and this was an embarrassing mistake) that the Coming of Christ back to earth was not very far away. Not tomorrow, perhaps, but soonish. This had some repercussions, as can be read, in the differences between Thessalonians 1 and 2, both written from Athens when he must have been depressed at the lack of success among the pagan philosophers. It looked as though there had been talk of backsliding in Thessalonica among the easygoing idol worshippers, on whom the idea of a single God had not impinged until the exposure to Paul's teachings. So the Second Epistle contains some gentle wrist slapping. Reading between the lines they were under the impression that Paul had promised that the end of the world was nigh; Christ was coming and they would soon be in Paradise with God. There was no need to work, then, just take things easy.

But Paul wrote:

'For even when we were with you, this we commanded you that if any would not work, neither should he eat. For we hear that there are some which walk among you disorderly, working not at all, but are busybodies. Now them that are such we command and exhort by ourLord Jesus Christ, That with quietness they work and eat their own bread.'

This does not suggest that Paul stayed there only two weeks, but long enough to be satisfied that reliable converts had been made. It also suggests the stay was long enough for Paul to work at his trade of tentmaker. Thessalonica was a large, thriving seaport with a strong Roman presence.

Leaving Thessalonica largely unscathed they went to Beroea and again entered the synagogue, where the Jews were rather more kindly. Before long the hostile Jews from Thessalonika arrived to harass them again. The stay was short and Paul left by sea for Athens, leaving Silas and Timothy behind in Beroea, though they rejoined him there later. Athens was two hundred and fifty miles to the South West.

Athens, however you looked at it, must have been considered by Paul to be the place in which he met his match;

and his worst failure. The Athenians did not flog him or put him in prison, they did something worse. They mocked him. 'Who is this babbler?' they said. He was trying to punch above his weight, a minnow amongst sharks. But the scholars, schooled in the philosophical dialogues of Plato, Xenophon, Aristotle and Socrates regarded him at best with amusement and at worst with contempt. He spoke to a great audience at the Areopagus, a rocky outcrop on the Acropolis, better known as the hill of Mars. How the audience received him is not reported. In silence? With rowdyness? Who knows? Paul's pride must have been hurt. Floggings he could take, prison was no great trial, but indifference? He rarely met with that. Converts were few in this greatest city of Eastern Europe, neither Jew nor Gentile. Two names are mentioned, Dionysius the Areopagite, and a woman named Damaris, but they never appear again either in Acts or the Epistles.

It would not have gone unnoticed that Paul never wrote a letter or an Epistle to the Athenians, nor did he ever return. Nevertheless, he had the last laugh, even if posthumously. Under pressure from the Emperor Constantine, two hundred and seventy years later, Athens succumbed, somewhat plaintively, to Christianity. I wonder if 'the babbler, Paul' was remembered? The worship of Zeus, Apollo and Jupiter was not wholly destroyed and continued until Justinian closed the pagan schools in 529 A.D.

Corinth, about thirty miles West of Athens, welcomed Paul along with Silas and Timothy, who had rejoined him. He was fortunate to meet Aquila, a Jew from Pontus, and his wife, Priscilla, recently expelled from Rome during one of the periodic Jewish purges. In this case the instigator was the Emperor Claudius. Paul was doubly fortunate in that they were tentmakers also and formed a strong rapport with him.

Athens may have been a failure but Corinth was an outstanding success. But then at Athens he was trying to convert the rich and famous, at Corinth, the proletariat. There was, not unexpectedly, trouble with the Jews, though he preached in the synagogue many times. Brave and pigheaded as ever he ended up by insulting them in the usual way: accusing them of blasphemy, and then marching out. As he says 'Henceforth I will go unto the Gentiles.' Still, according to Luke, he baptised Crispus, chief ruler of the synagogue. 'Man', said Job, 'is born to trouble, as the sparks fly upwards.' How shrewd was Job, and what an example of 'man' was Paul.

He may have been finished with the Jews but they were not finished with him. Greatly resentful of his actions they brought him to the Tribunal, presided over by Gallio, Pro-Consul of Achaia which included Corinth. Gallio, member of an aristocratic Roman family and brother of Seneca, was Pro-Consul during 50–51 A.D., which fixes Paul's time in Corinth accurately. He was having none of it, and told the Jews that Paul had broken no Roman law and rejected the charge. One would have thought that Paul in his guise of 'all things to all men' would have pleaded his Roman citizenship in front of Gallio, but he did not. His friends, the Greeks (and, presumably, converts) lent some colour to the proceedings by taking Sosthenes,the new ruler of the synagogue (presumably the job vacated by Crispus) and giving him a beating in Gallio's own court.

Paul , no doubt greatly pleased to avoid a flogging for once, stayed in Corinth for eighteen months, preaching successfully and earning good money at the tentmakers craft. He then left, taking Aquila and Priscilla , vowing to come back, and took ship to Ephesus; then Caesarea with a brief look in at Jerusalem; then by land back to Antioch, which ended his second missionary journey. His stay in Corinth, according to Acts, was one long success story; but was it? It would be useful to read his two Epistles to the Corinthians. These contain some glorious prose, such as:

> '*Though I speak with the tongues of men and of angels and have not charity, I am become as sounding brass or a tinkling cymbal.*'

and

> '*When I was a child I spoke as a child, I understood as a child, I thought as a child. But when I became a man I put away childish things.*'

But there is much that has no mention in Acts. Paul was greatly troubled. Strangely, these Epistles were written from Phillipi, presumably when he was there during the third journey. The writers of the first were Fortunatus, Achaicus and Timotheus, and Titus and Lucas wrote the second. To whom they were written at Corinth is not said. Paul had good reason to be concerned. The gathering, or 'church', he had confidently left behind had fallen apart into factions, all claiming allegiance to Paul and faith in Christ, but Paul's teaching must have been indifferent to result in the following competing sects:

- The Paulines (presumably those who had understood perfectly)
- The Cephas (Peter) party (down from Jerusalem?)
- Apollus the Alexandrene Jew preaching belief in John the Baptist
- Those who claimed they belonged to Christ through one to one contact (early gnosticism).

Sweetness and light must have been in very short supply in Corinth after Paul left. He must have gone beserk at the disturbing news filtering through to him about the lewd practices among those he had left behind, confident in the perfect ways of Christ, as taught to them by His Apostle Paul. These two Epistles, severely critical of their reported behaviour, encapsulate the complete canon of his teachings during the eighteen months he was with them. Indeed, they contained strictures he would not have felt necessary to discuss with them face to face: drunkeness, fornication, adultery, incest, effeminacy and self abuse.

'It is reported commonly that there is fornication among you; and such fornication as is not so much as named among the Gentiles,that one should have his father's wife.' (1 Corinth 5:1)

Despite his personal preference for celibacy, he felt constrained to advocate marriage if it meant the avoidance of fornication.

'But if they cannot contain let them marry. For it is better to marry than to burn.' (1 Corinthians 7:9)

Strangest of all, he thought it necessary to remind them of what he must have hammered at them face to face many times:

'But if there be no resurrection of the dead, then is Christ not risen and if Christ is not risen, then is our preaching vain and your faith also is vain.' (1 Corinthians 15:13–14)

and there is much more of the same in these Epistles. Paul must have wondered if the people of Corinth, that polyglot of tradesmen, soldiers, mystics and idol worshippers, had understood a single word of his sermons. He must have been terribly hurt, and it shows, as he pours out his heart. Of the thirteen Epistles the two to the Corinthians measure by volume more than one third of the total, and he must have had some doubt about the quality of his ministry.

The four factions, especially the Cephas Party, were lawyer dominated; still wedded to circumcision, the dietary laws and the Nazarenes. What he thought was a united church had become disunited, reminiscent of the multitude of schisms that were to tear the Church apart until the sixth century. Having written of his sufferings in proclaiming the Word of Christ, how he must have thought sometimes he was doing too much for too little reward.

'Of the Jews, five times received I forty stripes save one. Thrice was I beaten with rods; once was I stoned. Thrice I suffered shipwreck; a night and a day have I been in the deep.'
(2 Corinthians 11:20–25)

It is not known, certainly not from Acts, whether or not he ever returned to Corinth, but he says in 2 Corinthians 'This is the third time I am coming to you.' Whether he means in the flesh or through the two Epistles is not clear.

11

PAUL'S THIRD
MISSIONARY JOURNEY

'Fight the good fight; lay hold on eternal life.'

This third journey is considered to have started in
Antioch, after the brief stay in Palestine, though he did not
stay long. His companions are not named either but, together, they would have visited those places in which he
had preached during the first journey after leaving Cyprus,
to carry out a sort of audit on the lasting effects of his
preaching. These places would have included Derbe,
Lystra, Iconidium and Pisidian Antioch. But his main ob-
jective was Ephesus. That great seaport, in what is now
South West Turkey, acted like a magnet on Paul. It was
large and wealthy, full of pagans and other Gentiles. A pro-
fundity of Jews, of course, but he regarded *them* as the
greatest challenge, even though he had promised to keep
away from the circumcised. Ephesus was often spoken of,
more than Palestine, as the birthplace of Christianity, if
only because Paul stayed there more than three years in
this his second visit; longer than he ever spent in Antioch.
His principal enemies there, or, more accurately, his theological competitors, were not the Jews or the Jewish converts to Christ, but the local popular Gods of antiquity.
These offered universal magic and nostrums to cure just
about everything, while presided over by a priesthood of
the old religions with whom the people felt comfortable.

The importance of Ephesus owes much to Luke; supposedly a citizen and doctor of that city. At least according to Eusebius who wrote it in the fourth century. From whence he got his information is unknown. Luke's origins are not stated anywhere in the New Testament but Eusebius credits him with writing the Gospel of St. Luke and Acts.

The most important of Ephesus's pagan deities was Artemis (Diana to the Romans) and worship of her was very big business indeed. She was local to Galatia; not to be confused with Diana of the Athenian Greeks, the virgin huntress. They were distinctly different: Diana of the Ephesians was a fertility goddess whose statues were carved with many breasts, and the source of many magic powers. It was thought no surprise when the area converted to Christianity, the cult of Diana was simply transferred to the Mother of Jesus.

Lacking the cynicism of Athens, Paul expected an easier ride in Ephesus and more converts; and, rioting apart, he was successful. More easygoing, less concerned with phylosophical arguments, the people were not averse to adding another God to their pantheon of idols. To stay there more than two years was an acknowledgement of success. His task was made easier as he was not troubled by existing converts from Judaism to give him grief over the dietary laws and circumcision. Gentile converts were made in satisfying numbers.

In the early days he tried his luck in the synagogues as always, but the usual quarrels ensued and he moved out, to one Tyrranus, supposedly a wealthy Gentile, and preached from his house every day. Before long Paul, like the old gods, was being credited with magic, even miraculous powers of healing. What a paradox; Paul's success as an evangelist of the one and only God may been been due to the people's belief in Him as a magician. It was, of course, His curing of the sick and the resurrecting of the dead (Lazarus, brother of Mary and Martha) that made the name of Jesus famous in the hills of Galilee, though with no help from local deities.

There was, of course, some trouble, though not of Paul's making. The move away from the worship of Diana et al played havoc with the sales of images and souvenirs of the goddess made by the silversmith Demetrius and his fellow craftsmen. The trouble was one of commerce rather than theology. Presumably, in the fullness of time and pragmatism, your sturdy capitalist would have adjusted to a change in fashion and been just as ready to sell images of Christ and, later, much later, pictures of the Virgin Mary. They did at Lourdes in France and Knock in Ireland when busts of the Roman emperor were not exactly selling like hot cakes.

Anyway, Demetrius and his mates were set on trouble making, egged on by the usual subversives, and a huge meeting was called in the vast amphitheatre, and a couple of Paul's companions were dragged there and roughed up. A man named Alexander wanted to give a speech but, when exposed as a Jew, the crowd shouted him down. Paul, fearless and foolish as ever wanted to address the huge multitude but was dissuaded from doing so. There is a story put together by Pauline scholars that he *did* spend a fair time in prison while in Ephesus, but neither Paul in his Epistle to the Ephesians nor Luke in Acts, mentions it. It may be the reason why he never went back; fear of further imprisonment. Anyway the cult of Artemis continued for at least two hundred years after Paul, and the events at Ephesus, more than anywhere, illustrate the muscular nature of religious disputation, and it got worse through the centuries. He now leaves by sea for Macedonia taking some new faces with him, Sopator and Aristarchos, the pair dragged to the ampitheatre and beaten up. They landed at Phillipi where Paul stayed three months, during which time they checked up on the previous visits made to Thessalonica, Beroia and, possibly, Corinth.

Later they sail back to Troas, where the party splits, some going by sea down the coast as far as Samos. Paul alone goes by land to Ephesus but does not enter the town. He sends for the elders and delivers a powerful lecture, telling them how to behave, saying he was en route to Jerusalem. He also said something that has excited scholars until the present day, which can only be understood as a farewell speech. Paul is made to say:

> *'And now behold, I know that ye all among whom I have gone preaching the Kingdom of God, shall see my face no more.'*
> *(Acts 20:25)*

A common belief is that the author, (Luke?), did not write these words while Paul was still alive. If so, Acts could not have been completed before his death.

He then sailed down the coast to Parara; then across the open sea, leaving Cyprus on the port side, and on to Tyre. There, some disciples warned him, having been spoken to by the Spirit, not to go to Jerusalem. Like the address to the elders of Ephesus, this is considered to prepare everybody for the shattering events forecast to take place in Jerusalem, and then in Rome.

The day of reckoning is approaching. Paul and his party land at Caesarea where a prophet, Agabus, coming from Judea, warns him not to go on, as in Jerusalem the Jews will deliver him into the hands of the Gentiles, by which one supposes is meant to be the Romans. 'Splendid', Paul must have thought, 'Just what I want.'

12

ARRIVEDERCI JERUSALEM

'If God be with us, who can be against us?'

Paul meets James and the elders (but not Peter). The meeting seems amiable enough but he is asked to give evidence that he is still a practising Jew by paying the expenses, and looking after, four men, presumably Jewish Christians, who required re-purification in the Temple. They are members of a strange ascetic Jewish sect called Nazirites who forswear all products of the grape, as well as other pleasant things. All have broken their vows in some way, hence the need to be re-purified. Now here is a strange thing. In Ephesus, Antioch, Lystra and other places Paul would rant and rave against the Law, but in Jerusalem with the elders he is a pussy cat. Before he can give this demonstration of religious soundness, there is trouble with a gathering of Jews down from Ephesus, who accuse him of bringing a Greek Ephesian, by name Trophimus and a Gentile, into the area forbidden to non-Jews, and thus profaning the Holy Place. This was regarded as a crime so foul that there was a notice reading 'No foreigner is to pass within the railing and enclosure around the Temple on pain of death'. Moreover the Romans were prepared to allow the Jewish authorities to execute a lawbreaker, even if he was a Roman.

There was the customary riot which always followed Paul as night follows day and the crowd wanted to kill him; even though he had not brought Trophimus into the forbidden zone. He was brought to the Roman soldiers for arrest, and they took him to the commander, who *may* have commanded a cohort of some eight hundred to a thousand soldiers. He was surprised when Paul addressed him in Greek and allowed him to address the hostile, shouting crowd, from the steps leading into the jail of the Antonia fortress, which he did in the common tongue of Aramaic, *not* Hebrew. He proclaimed his Jewishness; born a Jew in Tarsus, no mean city; brought up in Jerusalem, he had studied the Law at the feet of the great teacher Gamiliel, and was a Pharisee.

He narrates his persecution of the early Jesus followers, his apocalypse on the Damascus Road; his appointment direct from God to carry out a mission to the Gentiles. In short, he was just as devout a Jew as they were, but he could hardly disobey a direct order from God to preach to the Gentiles. This went down like a lead balloon and the commander, to avoid further disorder, decided to examine him with a flogging, though thrashing somebody to extract information might be thought curious, even lacking in subtlety. Then Paul played his 'I am a Roman' card. 'You can't flog a Roman citizen,' he said. He and Silas had used this ploy successfully to avoid a beating in Phillipi. The Roman governor was astounded. He had just heard this man proclaim himself a Jew, and suddenly he is a Roman citizen. This worried him for he had had to *buy* his citizenship 'for a great price', unlike Luke's claim that Paul was born a Roman. This was almost certainly untrue as there is evidence to suggest that his father or grandfather had purchased Roman citizenship in Tarsus. Worried, the commander decided to play safe; it was dangerous to flog Paul who, moreover, had not been found guilty of any offence. Having escaped the scourging Paul is released to be brought before the entire council of the Sanhedrin.

Almost before he can speak Ananias, the High Priest, ordered him to be struck on the mouth. Paul complained and accused Ananias not of judging him according to the Law, but of striking him which was *against* the Law. He might also have said, as he did not hesitate to say to the Roman commander, 'How dare you, a Jew, strike a Roman citizen?' Instead, and it sometimes makes me feel that Paul suffered from temporary madness, he caused a quarrel to break out between the Sadducees, who did not believe in resurrection of the body and the Holy Spirit, and the Pharisees who believed in both; as did Paul, himself a Pharisee. *They* agreed with him, of course, and said that if Paul had had a message from God, let us not fight against God. Violence broke out, and Paul had to be arrested again by the Romans for his own safety and on the orders of the commander, a Tribune by rank and with the name of Lysias (a Greek name), and again confined to prison.

What was Paul's game? Did he *want* to be arrested, persecuted, flogged, threatened by the Jews with death, and not for the first time? Why did he ignore the warning given at Tyre not to go to Jerusalem? Why, when in the house of Philip in Caesarea, did he think so little of the highly respected prophet Agabus who warned him not to continue? Surely not in order to take alms to the poor? The others, Timothy or Barnabus for example, could have done that. Rome was his final destination ,(I think we can forget about Spain), and there were plenty of boats going there, not to mention the splendid network of Roman roads extending from Antioch, across Greece and the Balkans to the Adriatic Sea.

Was he hoping that by creating conflict, turmoil and riots

involving the Sanhedrin, the Jesus followers of Peter and James the brother of Jesus, and others (there were plenty of others), while claiming on one hand to be a devout Jew, and on the other a loyal Roman, he could put himself so much in the public eye, especially with the highest of Roman authorities, he might be helped on his way to Rome? This was a terrible risk but Paul was nothing if not a risk taker.

Paul had preferred on arrival in Jerusalem to lodge with Mnason, a Cypriot, Gentile and convert, rather than with the Jesus followers. (That would not have passed unnoticed.) The elders of the Jerusalem Church did not entirely trust him, and Peter was not in sight. James praised him for his good work among the Gentiles, but chided him with trying to persuade the Jews among the Diaspora in Asia not to circumcise their children, and preaching generally the irrelevance of circumcision and the absurdities of the dietary laws.

Paul *knew* that God had decided that after two thousand years the Mosaic Law and the Pentateuch had run their course, that his people must be inclusive *not* exclusive. As Paul wrote to the Galatians:

> 'There is neither *Jew* nor *Greek, there is neither bond nor free; there is neither male nor female: For ye are all one in Christ Jesus.' (Gal. 3:28)*

He must also have felt a measure of failure thus far in his mission among the Jews and Gentiles. He had failed to convince them that to be received by God it was only necessary to have faith in Christ Crucified. It was as simple as that; nothing else needed to be done; so taught and *thought* Paul. Simple it might have seemed; easy it was not. The devout Jew thought it encouraged immorality and lack of responsibility. The Gentile thought it meant they could do as they wanted, act as they wanted, because if they had faith and prayed for forgiveness God would forgive them – however heinous, however monstrous, their actions.

He had said goodbye to the Ephesians. He had been saddened by the shallowness of his success with the Corinthians, and with the Thessalonians. (Jesus' parable of the sower who went forth to sow comes to mind.) Antioch was, perhaps, a success story, but he had the most terrible rows there, e.g., the one with Peter. Neither were the Galatians his favourite pupils. Taking a long hard look at his mission, and being very self critical, he might have drawn the conclusion that his mission of Christ's Apostle to the Gentiles needed the greater communities outside Palestine and Asia Minor, i.e., Rome, untainted by the Jewish Law.

Paul had believed, beyond a peradventure, that the world as it was before the Crucifixion was coming to an end. Christ would be returning among them, and soon. He would come to separate the sheep from the goats, the just from the unjust, the fornicators from the chaste. But this had been his belief for twenty years, and his ministry had achieved only success in part. *Was* Christ coming?

Paul was now safe in prison; then two odd things happened. Out of the blue comes news that he has family in Jerusalem. This was not previously reported by Luke in Acts, nor by Paul himself, but it was very convenient to what followed. Apparently, he had a sister here with a son, his nephew. The boy had become privy to information that a band of fanatical Jews, some forty or so, had approached the chief priests saying they had sworn a great oath not to eat or drink until they had killed Paul. This they promised to do the next day, if Paul could be brought out of prison for further examination. The boy went to see him and told him of the plot. Paul told his centurion gaoler and asked him to take the boy to Claudius Lysias, the commander, and report the plot to *him*. Having played their part in this drama, sister and nephew dissolve into history.

Now for the second, quite astoundingly odd, event. Lysias was so disturbed by the news that he sends Paul, a prisoner of modest importance, under a guard of seventy cavalry, two hundred infantry and two hundred spearsmen, four hundred and seventy men, in the middle of the night, to Caesarea for examination and the protection of Felix the Governor.

It might just as well have been Felix the cat. At Antipas, forty miles en route, the foot soldiers return to Jerusalem and the cavalry complete the twenty miles to the Governor's Palace. Now, I don't know the per diem rate for a Roman soldier, or, for that matter, an officer. But if Lysias took the decision off his own bat, without reference to his superiors, to undertake the enormous expense of transporting Paul to Ceasarea, about a five to six day return journey for the troops, he would have been in deep trouble. Four hundred and seventy soldiers is half a cohort of five hundred to a thousand soldiers. Jerusalem may have been emptied to provide Paul's escort. He sent a covering letter to Felix ex-plaining what he had done which may have been an attempt to justify his action.

Covering letter? How could Luke, many years later, have had access to the private papers of a high ranking Roman officer? If true it may have been Luke's last act to build up Paul as a significant figure in the eyes of Caesar. Luke, or whoever wrote Acts, (its authorship has been disputed by the scholars over many years), never lost an opportunity to build up Paul as a Christian folk hero, somebody on whom the Romans could depend, and to denigrate the Jews as a quarrelsome, and at times, seditious people, responsible for most of the trouble in Jerusalem. Paul was never to see the city again.

After five days Ananias, the High Priest, came with a party, including, it says an orator, Tertullus, to plead the Jewish case against Paul, of sedition, among other crimes, and including blasphemy. The latter charge, of course, was of no interest to Felix, it lay outside the jurisdiction of Rome, and the sedition charge he dismissed out of hand. So, not wishing to upset the Jews, he was a corrupt man, always on the lookout for a bribe, he did not exactly release Paul, or imprison him. He was kept on a sort of loose rein, for two years. The High Priest, Ananias, went back home with a flea in his ear. Felix was replaced with Festus. Interestingly , Felix did not think the case against Paul strong enough to place him before his immediate superior, the Governor of Syria. This also throws doubt on the bringing of him at great cost to Caesarea.

Festus *also* is anxious not to upset the Jews. This feeling seemed to be general among Roman governors and procurators. 'Don't upset the Jews; riots are costly and, on my record, will not help me in Rome.' He *also* found no fault in Paul; though he suggested a trial back in Jerusalem. That was the last thing Paul wanted and he appealed to be heard before Ceasar. Festus was not disposed to take summary action against him in the absence of evidence that would stand up in court, and suggested he should appear before his friend, Agrippa, King of Lebanon, who just happened to be on a state visit to Caesarea. Agrippa II was a louche, liberal sort of man; brought up in Rome and well schooled in its statecraft and its easygoing, aristocratic way of life.

So they met, and spoke together in Greek, the language of upperclass Rome. Paul spoke to him, Jew to Jew, who would fully understand the trials, floggings and tribulations he had undergone in Jerusalem and elsewhere. He flattered Agrippa enormously in saying 'I know thee to be expert in all customs and questions which are among the Jews.' Agrippa must have liked him for he said 'Almost thou persuadest me to be a Christian.' This, after Paul had recited the events of his Apocalypse on the Damascus Road and Christ's appointment of him as Apostle to the Gentiles.

Then Agrippa said to Festus:

> *'This man might have been set at liberty, if he had not appealed unto Ceasar.' (Acts 27:32)*

This is a remark worthy of the Oracle at Delphi. What did Agrippa mean? Did he think that Paul, considered innocent by Claudius Lysias, Felix, Festus and himself, might be found guilty in Rome?

Paul had got his way.

GAME, SET AND MATCH TO PAUL.

13

BUONVENUTO ROMA

'Know we not that a litle leaven leaveneth the whole lump?'

The die was cast,and Paul, along with the other two hundred and seventy five prisoners, were delivered to the chief guard, the centurion Julius, of the cohort with the name Augustus. The ship, called Adramyttium, was in transit on its way to Myra, a port in Lydia.The next day they touched Sidon where Julius allowed Paul ashore to see his friends, converts from a previous voyage. This privilege is indicative that Paul *and* his friends were in a special category of prisoners, if they were prisoners at all.

At Myra Julius found one of those huge Alexandrian grain ships which plied several times a year to Rome in the sailing season, to feed the nine hundred thousand inhabitants, which included three hundred thousand slaves. That was the estimated population in the first century A.D. Egypt was just *one* of the bread baskets which fed Rome.The Emperor Augustus in the fifty five years or so of his reign gave contracts to private shippers to collect and deliver one hundred and forty thousand tons of wheat , i.e,. about two thousand four hundred and fifty tons a year. The boats were probably purpose built grain carriers of considerable capacity. The harvest was gathered in June and, with a suitable weather window of only five months before sailing became dangerous if not impossible, it must have taken at least four ships, at two return journeys each, to deliver Rome's wheat requirement.

And then, of course, there were the passengers. I wonder if the captain of the grain ship was astonished when Julius asked him for two hundred and seventy six singles to Rome please? And how did he pay? Allowing for the capricious nature of the winds, and primitive navigation methods, the journey could hardly have been less than two thousand miles, taking how long? Three weeks? Four weeks? I put this question while trying to imagine how much food and water would have been necessary to succour two hundred and seventy six prisoners plus the crew. I then wondered, was the ship's captain prepared to receive this unexpected load?

The only evidence of this last voyage of Paul is that contained in Acts Chapters 27/28. And it is surely the most widely reported voyage and shipwreck in marine history. Only in Acts and nowhere else can you read about it. The learned divines, the theological giants scribbling away (as King George III said of Edward Gibbon) in their musty scriptoria, inserting a comma during the morning, and taking it out in the afternoon, must have been at their wits end to inflate Acts account. Some of them, greatly daring, even posed the question, rhetorically of course, 'Did Paul *make* the voyage? There are certainly those who write that Luke shared the voyage with him. This they base, one supposes, on the Author of Acts who says 'At the next day we touched at Sidon.' They then assume that if Acts *was* written by Luke, then when the word 'we' is used Luke *must* have been with him. But Luke's name is *never* mentioned in Acts, though Aristarchus of Thessalonica, a Macedonian and companion of Paul, was on the ship

But for every Paulist who believes Luke was on the ship there is a doubter who does not. And if he was not, was he also not with him in Rome? But if he was on the ship it would explain the splendid piece of prose describing the weather, the storms and the shipwreck. Then again, if Luke didn't write it, who did?.

Acts gives no month of departure from Caesarea but September is considered a likely month. Working backwards from Myra with 'many days' to the Fair Havens in South West Crete, it was probably in late October, or even November, when the ship's captain headed West into dangerous seas, against the advice of Paul. During this perilous time he is depicted as a tower of strength,, a man of authority, giving advice which was listened to courteously by both Lucius and the captain. Neither of them heeded his advice, of course, but nor was he chucked overboard as an interfering, ignorant landlubber. It could have happened? No, it could not; this story is important in the presenting of Paul as a man of influence; listened to; sometimes deferred to; always respected. A man on his way to Rome, perhaps even to confront the Emperor. The character creation continues, after the casting onto the shore of Malta in raging seas, with two stories. The venomous snake, a viper which fastens itself to his hand but does not harm him, and the curing from 'a fever and a bloody flux' of the father of the island's 'leading man, Publius.' This may lack the miraculous resurrection from the dead of Lazarus but every little helps in the creation of Paul as a man who could cure the sick, the halt and the lame. On such things the reputation of a first century A.D. mystic depended. During the Winter spent on Malta the writer of Acts continues to speak of 'we' and 'us' as further evidence that Luke was with Paul.

After three months Paul and *all* the prisoners, for none were said to have died in the shipwreck, boarded a ship out of Alexandria bound for Italy. They landed at Syracusa on the East coast of Sicily where they stayed three days and then went on to Rhegium, modern day Reggio di Calabria, across the Straits of Messina on the toe of Italy, from where a favourable wind took them to Puteoli in two days. The modern name is Pozzuoli, on the North coast of Naples Bay. There, Paul is said to have found Christian brethren; not surprising considering the excellent maritime communications of the day. And, of course, Putuoli was a considerable port and town at which many ships arrived from the Middle East, carrying the corn of Egypt and cosmopolitan peoples of many nationalities.

They were now on the final leg of this epic journey. The Appian Way led North to Rome, a distance of about one hundred and thirty miles, and Paul and his friends, along with the escort, would have taken about six days to reach the gates of the greatest city in the world (unless they dallied on the way) and in Rome the escort handed them over to the military authority.

After three days he 'Called the chiefs of the Jews together' and told them his story, from prison in Jerusalem to trials in Caesarea, where his innocence before Felix, Festus and the Jewish King, Agrippa, was accepted.; and his request to be sent to Rome to appeal to the Emperor. The Jews listened patiently, saying they had received no news about him from Jerusalem, certainly nothing bad. Saying also that the teachings of Jesus were believed by some, but not by most. Paul seems to have bridled at this and, in his inimitable way, on the basis that those who are not one hundred per cent for me are against me, reproached them by quoting a passage from Isaiah, the prophet to our forefathers:

'Hearing you shall hear, and shall not understand. And seeing ye shall see, and not perceive.'

And so on.

Paul failed again, but he should not have been talking to the leading Jews in Rome in this manner. Not if he was to pay more than lip service to the Agreement reached in Jerusalem with Peter and James the brother of Jesus, by which Paul would be the Apostle to the Gentiles and they the Apostles to the Circumcision. He is then said to have spent two years preaching without let or hindrance.

Then the light flickers, the screen goes blank and history, unlike tradition, has nothing more to add to the life of Paul the Apostle.

14

PAUL IN ROME

'I therefore, the prisoner of the Lord, beseech you that you walk worthy of the vocation wherewith ye are called.'

Was he there? Some scholars express doubts; but the body of evidence in favour of his being there is not small. Though he could not have arrived before 58 A.D., if the chronology of Acts is examined; and it must have been 8–10 years after he wrote the Epistles to the Romans from Corinth, where he was for eighteen months. But to whom was it addressed, converts, of course, but Gentiles or 'God Fearers'? 'God Fearers', those non-Jews attracted to Judaism, attended the synagogue but neither kept the dietary laws nor were they circumcised. These had provided many converts by way of Jesus' Apostles. Priscilla and Aquilla, Paul's converts from Corinth, though earlier expelled from Rome by the Emperor Claudius as Jews, were such as Paul would have been addressing. Though later they returned to Rome when it was safe to do so, and are mentioned in the Epistle to the Romans. He had, of course, a great difference of opinion with the God Fearers; e.g., with Barnabus and John Mark, after the first missionary journey to Cyprus. Which might explain Paul's unusual, indeed out of character, colciliatory composition of much of this Epistle.

Romans is considered to be his masterpiece of epistolary style. The content, now persuasive, now congratulatory; gracefully reports much of his ministry; longing, and promising to join them. It was philosophical in tone, condemnatory of unusual and vicious sexual practices among men with men, and women with women, not forgetting to be reproachful of circumcision, without ranting against it, as he frequently did in Antioch, Ephesus and other places; especially in the synagogues. Though he does not mention persuading Timothy to undergo the painful mutilation of circumcision in Lystra, purely for pragmatic, one might almost say political, convenience.

He did not forget his strictures on the Mosaic Law. It had served God's purpose for two thousand years but it had never been God's will that it should be exclusive to the Jews. The Gentiles were never to be excluded for ever; and the time had come to bring them into the fold. And as he had done many times, he leaned on Abraham to justify his evangelism among the Gentiles. But was he addressing the Gentiles and the God Fearers? The more one reads Romans, there is more than a hint that he is addressing Roman Jews rather than Roman Gentiles. I have wondered if Paul had considered the converting of Gentiles hardly stretched his gift of religious persuasion; but the Jews, his own people! To convert them, *that* would be a triumph. It is of such startling clarity and composition; Christ's Apostle to the Gentiles he may have been, but what if his real target was the Mosaic Law itself?

But there is one verse (Chapter 13:1), that explodes like a hand grenade in a crowded room, which dominated the actions of the high powered priestly hierarchy, and the secular and civil authorities which emerge from Constantine the Great's making Christianity the religion of the Roman Empire. A verse that has troubled scholars to the present day:

*'Let every soul be subject unto the higher power. For there is no
power but of God. The powers that be are ordained of God.'*

Paul could not have deeply understood the enormity of this
instruction, for that is what it was, an instruction. He was
saying that however evil the action of those in authority, it
should be accepted without question by those under authority. For all power came from God alone. Thus was sanc-
tified for evermore, according to Paul, the injustice of a king
over his subjects, a slave owner over his slaves.

This verse could never have been spoken by Jesus and is
in stark contrast to the Magnificat of the Virgin Mary (Luke
1:52):

*'He has put down the mighty from their seats, and exalted
them of low degree.'*

What wars, what insurrections and bloody conflicts must
that instruction from Paul to the faithful have caused over
the centuries. Paul, in fact, had, with that verse in the Epistle
to the Romans, established *his* position in the eternal struggle on earth between the classes:

*'The rich man in his castle,
The poor man at his gate;
God made them high or lowly,
And order'd their estate.'*

So what did he do in Rome? He had lodgings for himself
and a Roman soldier to pay for and it is doubtful if he had
any money. Thanks be to God and his wise father, he had his
tent maker's trade and Nero's Rome would have offered
plenty of work for a craftsman. Paul would have had no

problem keeping body and soul together. Apart from that, and *that* is conjecture, how did he justify coming to Rome? Preaching, evangelising, haranguing the Jews in their synagogues, no doubt. Well, that again is conjecture; there is simply no record of Paul in Rome, except the Epistles. The New Testament records four written by him from Rome to his converts in various towns in Asia Minor and Greece. Thirteen, in fact, are accepted as written by him, but not the one to the Hebrews. A considerable body of scholars dispute the Pauline authorship of Thessalonians II and Ephesians. Some also doubt he wrote Collossians and Philippians. All but the most sceptical of modern scholars accept he wrote Romans, Galatians and Corinthians.

Now, who could these people be then that may, or may not, have forged eight of the thirteen, and why? They are unknown and short of an incredible find like the Dead Sea Scrolls they will remain so. It may well be that when they were gathered together, well into the third century, the compiler thought Paul's canon of scholarship rather thin, and decided, with the best of intentions, to thicken it up somewhat. No original manuscripts survive.

Luke, if we can believe Acts, and the voyage to Rome was supposed to be with him, (and, as back up to this, Luke is supposed to have been buried at Padua, three hundred miles North East of Rome). A prolific writer like Luke, one might reasonably suppose, would have written to this friend Theophilus or many others reporting on the splendid work his friend Paul was doing among the Roman Gentiles. And what about Peter? Eusebius (264–340 A.D.), Bishop of Caesarea, wrote with confidence from a position three hundred years or so after the events that Peter was the first Bishop of Rome from about 40 A.D. to 64 A.D. Would Paul, or Luke, or any one of many not have written to Jerusalem, or Antioch or to the many Gentile communities in Greece or Asia Minor with the good news?

Paul would have been there in a relatively calm period of Nero's reign. Nero only entered the more tabloid pages of Roman history through his savage and inhuman executions of Christians after the burning of the city. Those who were not crucified were covered in tar and burned alive as human torches in the Vatican Gardens. It was considered politically sensible by a tyrant to fasten blame for a catastrophe or crime of immense proportions on a convenient victim, lest the people fasten it on *him*. Scapegoats are never difficult to find; ask any Jew with a knowledge of his people's history. But in this case, despite the presence of many Jews, Nero chose the Christians. Everything was in their favour; there were not many of them; the survivors were unlikely to cause trouble; they were available and of no particular concern to the body of Roman citizenry. There is evidence that Nero had no particular dislike of the Christians. In common with most of the Emperors he was unconcerned who or what his subjects worshipped as long as they caused no trouble. Hence he sacrificed the Christians almost as an act of convenience. He knew nothing of Christianity. The unfortunate, murdered Christians were not martyrs, but victims.

How many innocents were sacrificed to create a Roman holiday, and which, save but for the use of the word 'martyr' would have been forgotten among the hundreds of massacres perpetrated by the Christian Churches against heretics, infidels and Jews. In Basle, Switzerland, September 1348, during the Black Death Plague which killed twenty five per cent of the European population, all the Jews who could be rounded up were put into wooden buildings and burned alive. In December the same year the Jews were burnt in Landsberg, Burren, Merringen and Lindau. In

January 1349 the same, at Freiburg im Breisgau, Ulm and Speyer. In February the Jews were slaughtered at Gotha, Eisenbach and Dresden. In March they were burnt at Worms, Baden and Erfurt. And why were the Jews killed? 'Because they had caused the Plague. And had they not killed our Lord Jesus Christ?' No matter that the plague killed even handedly, Jew alongside Gentile. Who remembers the Jews? And who forgets the Christians?

Other people he might have mentioned, had they been in Rome, were Peter's fellow Apostles, Andrew his brother, James and John the sons of Zebedee, Philip and Bartholemew, Matthew and Thomas, James the son of Alpheus, Simon the Canaanite and Mathias who replaced Judas Iscariot. Whatever happened to them in those tumultuous days and early years after the Crucifixion? Tradition has it (how very important is tradition in the Christian story) that Paul went to Spain; he spoke about it in several passages of the Epistles. Well, Spain had been a part of the Roman Empire for over four hundred years. If he *did* go he would have been fortunate to have survived a journey by land of over fifteen hundred miles in primitive, dangerous territory, and by sea an equally perilous voyage. The Mediterranean coast had been colonised by Greeks and others since 500 B.C., but it was sparsely populated. Why he should even have considered going is surprising; for Rome with its nine hundred thousand to two million or so people, including three hundred thousand slaves, (I treat these numbers with caution; no, not caution, but disbelief, they are always quoted – let us say that Rome in the first century had many people), would have provided a life time of conversion work; and the converted, especially the soldiers, would have taken his teachings of the Christian God to the four corners of the Empire.

If he did die in Rome in 60 A.D., why by execution? Why should the Roman authorities be concerned by yet another religious ranter. As long as Paul did not cause riots or dangerous disturbances in Rome, as he had in Jerusalem, Ephesus and other places, the Romans would not have cared. But, of course, Paul always *did* cause trouble; so perhaps he *did* lose his head. Anyway, a basilica was built in memory of his martyrdom some three hundred years later and it is called St. Paul without the Wall, (San Paolo Fuori le Mura). The tradition of his beheading was first recorded by Eusebius circa 350 A.D., who thus won the double of giving to a grateful world both the execution of Paul, and the Bishopric and execution of Peter in Rome.

There is another very puzzling fact which still remains unanswered. The book entitled 'The Destruction of the Jews' written by Josephus, describing the war on the Jews by the Emperor Titus 66–70 A.D., and at which Josephus was present, describes, in the greatest detail, how Jerusalem was razed to the ground, save a part of the Western Wall; and every Jew in the city slaughtered. This raises the question of the dating of Acts, and also the four Gospels. Mark, on which Matthew and Luke are considered to be based, is thought to have been written about 70 A.D. and Acts not before 70–80 A.D.; some say much later. This horrible catastrophe was the worst to hit the suffering Jews since the Babylonian Captivity. So, how could it have gone unmentioned in Acts and the Gospels, written beyond reasonable doubt after the event of the destruction of Jerusalem containing, as it did, the Temple, Herod's Palace and the Antonia Fortress? The greatest town in the known world flattened, greater even than Rome, and the writer of Acts didn't seem to know about it.

So, as far as Acts is concerned, or any other part of the

New Testament, Paul vanished in or about 60 A.D. An epic story that began with the martyrdom of Stephen and ended thirty years later with his disappearance in Rome. As Winston Churchill said of Russia, Paul was 'A riddle wrapped in a mystery inside an enigma'. Despite his belief that Christ would return to earth in his lifetime, he created a church without either walls or structure, strongly linked to Judaism, though denying the need for the Laws of Moses, and remained a Jew to the very end.

He lit a very long metaphorical fuse, attached to a metaphorical barrel of gunpowder that exploded in the sky to form a flaming cross at the Milvian Bridge in 312 A.D. near Rome. The Emperor Constantine saw the cross which bore the message 'In this, conquer', and, superstitious as were all Emperors, he took it as a good omen and went forth to defeat Maxinius to become sole Emperor in the West. And when he had finally killed all his enemies in both West and East he established Christianity as the State Religion, adding the caveat, 'I will make Christianity the footstool of my Empire'. What a splendid, and the first, example of the Church Militant. Bismarck, the German Chancellor in the nineteenth century, said 'The most significant event of the nineteenth century is that the Americans speak English.' Constantine's Adoption of Christianity was of equal importance in the fourth century.

The explosion may have taken two hundred and seventy years to detonate, but it flung the word of Paul and of Jesus's Nazarenes to the four corners of both the ancient and the modern worlds.

15

AFTER ROME AND
BEFORE CONSTANTINE

'For we brought nothing into this world;
and it is certain we can carry nothing out.'

It has been said, and perhaps Edward Gibbon's voice, in his 'Decline and Fall of the Roman Empire', spoke with clarity and scepticism, that 'It has been remarked with more ingenuity than truth that the virgin purity of the church was never violated by schism or heresy before the reign of Trajan and Hadrian, about one hundred years after the death of Christ.'. This may have been true but there was one event that must have struck terror, and horror, to all Jews and Christians throughout the Roman provinces of Asia Minor. The complete destruction of Jerusalem, hardly one stone left on another, in the War on the Jews (66–76 A.D.), carried out with great brutality by Titus and his legions. Most of the Jews who survived the slaughter joined the Diaspora of their people throughout Asia Minor and other places. Later, Hadrian put down another insurrection in Judea, and built a new city on Mount Sion which he named Aelia Capitolina. It was heavily garrisoned and Jews were denied entry.

James, the brother of Jesus, was stoned to death in 62 A.D. by order of the Sanhedrin, presumably for blasphemy, but more likely for political reasons. Note: the Pharisees were said to have defended him against the Sadducees who wanted him dead. But by far the saddest event was what happened to the Nazarines. Bereft of James' leadership, and he was one of the first fifteen Bishops of Jerusalem, all of whom were circumcised Jews, the Nazarines who had survived the slaughter during Jerusalem's destruction retired to the village of Pella, beyond Jordan. Marcus, their first Bishop in Pella ironically was a Gentile and under him they renounced the Mosaic Law, while maintaining the teachings of Jesus and his Apostles. After seventy years they spread towards Damascus and Aleppo, further North in Syria.

Their hatred of Paul and his Hellenism and anti-Jewish leanings was intense. His evangelism they regarded as destructive of the purity and Godliness of Jesus, and heretical. They, in truth, were considered by the Gentile converts as childlike rustics, and given the contemptuous name of Ebionites from the Hebrew word 'ebjonim', which, in Latin, means 'Poor devils'. Later they were called heretics which was like calling Jesus a heretic. Later still they were persecuted for treason. It could be said that the Jesus Church of Jerusalem was overwhelmed by the apostates from Greek polytheism who had come to the faith under the banner of Paul. It could be said that from this mixture of rootstock, Christianity offered itself to the world, aimed with the strength and morality of Judaism, but without its fetters. The destruction of Jerusalem effectively removed the Jesus Church from the map, in the spreading of Christianity to the outside world.

The quiescent period up to Hadrian was followed by furious religious activity, as the leaders appointed by Paul's pupils started to analyse his basic instructions concerning Christ, and God the Father. A breed of theological intellectuals was born which was both the saviour and curse of Christianity in the centuries to follow. Paul, when he quitted first his early stamping grounds, then this mortal coil, left a disorderly church or churches; largely devout, sometimes confused, but always ready to defend through argument, or force if need be, what they considered their particular version of the worship of Christ. There was chaos, with fights, murders and persecutions, all in the name of faith in Christ Crucified. For they all believed in that even if they had little else in common.

For at least the next three hundred and fifty years schisms and heresies abounded. Schismatics and heretics were the bane of orthodoxy. Each heresy was usually the brainchild of an individual, who could always start a splinter group. Although the Latin Church could sniff out a latent heresy, or group of schismatics, with the skill of a Customs and Excise hound sniffing cannabis, and ensure it was exterminated by expulsion or worse. But there were certain schisms which greatly destabilised the emerging shape of Christianity, and undoubtedly had a profound effect. Finally the Latin Church of the West, aided by Athanasius, Bishop of Alexandria, who swung the Council of Nicea (325 A.D.) their way, (Christ and God are the *same* substance; and the Trilogy of God, the Son and the Holy Ghost), felt safe, for the moment. But the East, Constantinople, Alexandria Antioch and other Greek influenced towns, had their own agendas.

A modern Christian finds difficulty in believing the goings on, antics and strange, wayward beliefs of the schismatics. Indeed, most church and chapel goers have neither knowledge or belief in them. But they are worth examination, if only to learn of the gullibility of people; a gullibility as strong in the twentyfirst century as in the first century A.D.

The DOCETES: They flourished widely but briefly in the early second century and were noted for the non-acceptance of the life of Jesus prior to his ministry. In particular, they did not accept the story of Mary's conception and the birth of Jesus. They maintained Jesus was divine only; not incarnate, no real body on earth; only a phantom body. All sensual aspects were disclaimed, maintaining that the Holy Ghost passed through Mary like a sunbeam through a glass window. Christ did not die on the cross because a God cannot die. Even those of the times, believing in miracles and resurrections as they did, found this heresy hard to swallow, and it finally faded away. Right and properly, for their name 'Docetes' means 'phantom' in Greek

The GNOSTICS: Gnosticism was a deadly serious concept and belief, and has frequently defied description. Did it precede Christianity or did it grow from it? It was certainly known before the birth of Jesus and was practised in the first and second centuries among early Christians, and survives to some extent among the Christian Copts of Egypt. Gnosticism was Hydra-headed, inclined to take parts of Christian belief and fasten them on to their own secret core of mysticism which was based on a dual world of good and evil, light and darkness. They scorned the Genesis account of the Creation, the Deity after the six days of labour, the Garden of Eden and much else of the Jewish Pentateuch. But, and this was an important 'But', it was their fundamental doctrine that Christ was the emanation of God on earth; the *Deus ex Machina'* to rescue mankind. Their influence on early Christianity was considerable; and Paul recognised the sinister influence of this esoterical sect and, more or less, accepted its presence. They were everywhere; in Asia, Egypt, Rome and even further West, and were not completely suppressed for many centuries, if at all.

The MONOPHYSITES: The name that is synonymous with this heresy is Nestorius, fifth century Patriarch of Constantinople, fortunate in only being banished for his sins to a monastery in Upper Egypt. With the Emperor Anastatius he denied that the Virgin Mary could truly be called the Mother of God, and thus emphasized the distinction of the earthly nature of Jesus and the divine nature of Christ after the resurrection. In this case, of course, he was at one with the Jews. 'There is but one God; no Trinity of God the Father, God the Son and God the Holy Ghost.'. It was this heresy that cleaved the Church from top to bottom, like a felling axe splitting a log.

Nestorius was a Syrian ecclesiastic, ascetic and devout, and it is generally considered that the monophysistic belief in the singularity of God which spread rapidly in Asia Minor, left the gate wide open for the rapid spread of the Islamic faith with *its* belief in one God, rejection of the Virgin Birth, the divinity of Christ and the Holy Ghost. The Monophysites were, in fact, early Muslims, and rejected much of Paul's teachings, while remaining devout Christians. They remain today as Copts in Egypt, in Armenia, Ethiopia and as Maronites in the Lebanon.

The DONATISTS: Donatus was a Numidian Bishop in North Africa, fourth century, in the region of Carthage. Their chief dogma was that the Christian Church was a society of holy people only, and mortal sinners were to be excluded. This exclusivity has its modern equivalents in many modern christian sects. Violence was likely to be used on reluctant acolytes.

This was, of course, the territory and period of St. Augustine, who was regarded as the genius of the orthodox Latin Church, and, after Paul, was considered the man who gave stable and permanent shape to Christianity in the West. In his youth he was a student of the Manicheans, the third century B.C. gnostic sect. As written earlier, gnosticism, though not Christian, had great influence on its development. How other could a man of Augustine's stature have been attracted to it? In Paul's day, and for centuries after, it was practised. Augustine did much to destroy the influence of Donatism; but it was a memorable schism which afflicted the African provinces until Christianity itself was extinguished by the armies of Islam in the seventh century. They did not dispute the Divinity of Christ, the Virgin Birth or the Trinity, the usual arguments of schismatics, but seemed to be a sect of bloodyminded Savanarolas, unable to accept the frailties of mankind.

ARIANISM: The originator of Arianism was Arius, an elder of the church of Alexandria in the fourth century. He maintained that the Father and Son were distinct beings; that the Son, though Divine, was not equal to the Father; that the Son had a state of existence prior to His appearance on earth, but not from eternity; that the Messiah (Christ) was not a real man but a Divine Being in a veil of flesh. Here one can detect the minor influence of the Docetes. The heresy was condemned by the Council of Nicea (325 A.D.), which upheld the orthodox view of Athanasius, that the Son was 'of the substance with the Father'. But this condemnation by no means wiped out Arianism.

Constantine's attitude to Christianity was benign; he affected none of the extreme hatreds of the competing sects for each other and was no philosopher like Julian, prepared or able to debate the esoteric nature of the Divinity. Arianism was widely supported in Constantinople, and though Constantine was won over at first by Athanasius and the orthodoxy, and ordered the exile of Eusebius, Bishop of Nicomedia, along with other leaders of Arianism, he later rescinded the exile; Eusebius returned and the Arians were once more supreme in Constantinople, and the rest of the Eastern Empire.

The part played by the Goths (Visigoths and Ostrogoths) is often neglected. They constantly swarmed over the Danube to the great irritation of, and danger to, the Roman legions. The Romans made slaves of the many prisoners of war who, almost by accident, renounced Paganism for Christianity – the Arian version. In the late fourth century and until the end of the sixth, they conquered finally the whole of the Roman Empire in Europe and brought Arianism to Gaul, much of Italy, and Spain. Happily, and without conflict, the Gothic Arians were won over to the orthodox Latin Church. Clearly the effect of Arianism was profound, took some three hundred years before its influence disappeared and, doubtless, continued to be practiced in remote places.

In retrospect, the schisms and the heresies read like the childish tantrums of adolescents. Yet their founders were highly intelligent people; but their lack of wisdom and their actions would have been anathema to Paul, who abhorred cruelty, hatred and intolerance. Looking at the names that emerge at the top of this dung heap, not one of them was worthy of Paul.

What did they argue about, incessantly, unendingly; and with Bishops, Archbishops and Greco-Roman politicians? Everbody was armed to the teeth, weapons of torture at the ready, to back up their version of the divine truth. They argued about:

- Was Jesus man or divine?
- Was the Son and God made of the same substance?
- Was God in three parts: God the Father, God the Son and God the Holy Ghost?
- Was Jesus a wraith, not flesh?
- Did Christ have a single nature but consisting of two natures?

- Did Christ have two natures but one will?
- Did God the Father exist before God the Son/

From Alexandria to Antioch, and in towns the length and breadth of Asia Minor, these abstractions were disputed at the cost of hundreds of thousands of lives. We all know the old joke of how many angels can sit on a pinhead. That was no joke in the second to the eighth century after Paul. Towns may have gone to war in disputation on it.

16

EMPEROR JULIAN
THE APOSTATE

'Unto the pure, all things are pure.'

Flavius Claudius Julianus, to give him all his names, was a nephew of Constantine the Great. On Constantine's death in 337 A.D. and the accession of his three sons as Caesars to the three parts of the Empire, there was a general massacre of the males of the younger line of the Flavian family. Cruel but fair as is sometimes said today of professional gangster families as they gun down their competitors. Only Julian and Gallus were spared, possibly on grounds of youth. If Constantine the Great had imbued any of the Christian virtues, particularly that of mercy, none had been inherited by his murderous sons. Julian, only five at the time, was traumatised by the murder of his father and other relatives, and, over the years and for the rest of his short life, developed a hatred of Christianity. From the age of about twelve he willingly submitted himself to the study of the old Greek philosophers, Plato, Socrates and others; and knowledge of the ancient Greek Gods; Zeus, Artemis and Apollo. There were quite a number of older men at court that still worshipped the Pagan Gods, and were well versed in the mystery cults. Julian was a voracious scholar. Constantine;, his older cousin, now Emperor of the whole empire, having murdered his two brothers, and likely himself to remain childless, trusted Julian just enough to make him Caesar in

Gaul, hoping he would prove a failure. To his surprise, and despite keeping Julian's army short of men, money and materials, the young Julian, a scholar, turned himself into a brilliant general, much loved by his legions, and was later considered the most successful general in Gaul and the Rhine since Julius Caesar; and the only scholar Emperor since Marcus Aurelius, two hundred years earlier. At the age of twenty nine, with Constantine deeply unpopular with the army, Julian by popular assent of both generals and soldiers was declared Emperor Augustus, and marched on Constantinople. At Sumian he declared himself a pagan, totally renouncing Christianity openly, intending to encourage a return to the old ways of worship and to re-open the old shrines in the Eastern Empire. He had never sought popularity nor encouraged rebellion against Constantine, who conveniently died, unusually for a Roman Emperor, in his bed. Julian was crowned Emperor in Constantinople. For the previous ten years he had been secretly worshipping at the ancient shrines in Antioch and Ephesus. During his short reign of twenty months he ruled with justice and wisdom, tolerating both Christians (known for some reason as Galileans) and Jews; openly encouraging a return to the ancient pagan religions of the previous fifteen hundred years. He re-opened the temples of Artemis, Apollo, Poseidon and Aphrodite in many towns throughout Asia Minor, where Paul had preached. And in Corinth and Athens. There was plenty of opposition, from the vast hierarchy of Christian Archbishops, Bishops and Patriarchs, but no violence.

He then led the army Eastwards, across the Euphrates and the Tigris to fight the Persians, a battle planned by Constantius, but with which Julian was in agreement. It had been festering for years, and Rome wanted to finish the Persians once and for all. There was a great victory, but on the way out of Persia, pursued by guerilla bands, he received a fatal spear wound. Later it was widely rumoured that he was killed by a plot among several of his Christian generals, secretly, for they feared the anger of the loyal legions; to whom Julian had presented a great victory. Dead at the age of thirty two.

It is anybody's guess what the effect of a long lived Julian would have had on a religion change in Europe. Julian the Apostate was the most tolerant of Emperors, even to Christians. An example of this was when he invited the priests of different Christian sects into the Palace, and politely expressed his wish that they should end their squabbles and allow each to follow his own beliefs, without hindrance or fear. In a Machiavellian way he thought that such freedom would only deepen their differences and he would not be faced by united opposition. He had found from experience that wild beasts are not as hostile to men as Christians to each other.

Julian uncovered many unpleasant abuses among the Christian clerics of the upper class, and he forbad them to sit as judges, or draw up wills for they took the inheritances of others and assigned the property to themselves. They were inclined to behave in the manner that Paul warned his converts against.

Edward Gibbon dates the untimely death of Julian when his task of re-establishing the worship of the old Pagan Gods was hardly begun, as the end of the Decline and the beginning of the Fall of the Roman Empire. The cause of which he attributes to the triumph of Pauline Theology. By an irony of fate the embalmed body of Julian the Apostate was borne by the grieving legions from Persia to Tarsus in Cilicia, the birthplace of Paul the Apostle.

17

THE PAULICIANS

'Faith is the substance of things hoped for,
the evidence of things not seen.'

The incomprehensible mysteries of the Incarnation and the Trinity dominated the Roman and Greek theologians for century after century; schism after schism. By the seventh century a certain passivity ruled the passions of dispute; and peace, though not amity, was in most places. The Pagans were keeping their heads below the parapet; the Jews were quiet and obscure; and the sects of Egypt and Syria were enjoying toleration under the Caliphs of Islam.

After six centuries of dissolute, quarrelsome and cruel patriachs, bishops and Emperors, all Christians of a sort since Constantine the Great, there emerged on the Asia Minor scene a man, by name Constantine, who seemed to have inherited many of Paul's virtues. Austere, simple in his requirements and chaste, he somehow came into possession of the complete New Testament. A rare gift since both the Latin and Greek priests abhorred the idea that it should be available for reading by laymen. Constantine was enthralled by the writings of Paul and, in a way, attached himself to his character; and saw himself as a spiritual descendent of Titus, Timothy, and the other Pauline converts. He quickly gathered together humble men and women like himself and together they gloried in their affinity with the Apostle to the Gentiles. The names of the apostles' churches were given to their congregations in Armenia and Cappodocia. After the sophisticated horrors of the previous centuries they chose to go back to the primitive Christianity of Paul; as their detractor quickly called it; and these, their enemies, called them contemptuously 'Paulicians'. This was too much, for the organised authority of both Latin and Greek hierarchies could never have permitted the Paulicians to survive; at least as members of yet another heretical sect.

Their enquiries into the life of Paul were done with pure love; though they were far from perfect; rejecting the two Epistles of Peter; and had contempt for the Old Testament, their creed of primitive christianity would be applauded by many modern day Protestants. They rejected the veneration of relics as false worship and the Cross was no more than a piece of wood. The bread and wine of the Mass was rejected; as was the immaculate and perpetual virginity of the mother of Christ. The saints and angels were no longer solicited as channels of intercession with God. In short, the Paulicians regarded the Word of the Gospel as simply faith in Christ and baptism; and were inclined to abolish all visible objects of worship. It is not surprising that they found the Orthodox Church's belief in the Trinity absurd.

Constantine's apostolic labours soon multiplied the number of his followers; and the number was swollen by many Catholics, Manicheans of Armenia, and remnants of the various Gnostic sects in the towns so diligently proselytised by Paul. They had no desire for the wealth and honours, the perks of office, so greedily sought by the Orthodox priesthood. The sect was loosely spread over Asia Minor and six of its largest congregations were near the churches to whom Paul had actually addressed his Epistles.

After twenty seven years, Sylvanus (for Constantine had changed his name to that of Paul's disciple) having left the protection and toleration of the Arab Caliphs, fell foul of Roman persecution. A Greek Minister, by name Simeon, equipped with legal and military authority, appeared at his house in Colonia, on the Southern shore of the Black Sea. He placed Sylvanus in front of his disciples and ordered them, on pain of death, to kill him. After a very long time one of them carried out the execution. Simeon, overcome by what he had ordered: the death of the spiritual father of these humble people, and observing the noble virtues of Sylvanus, joined the sect and in his turn became both missionary and martyr. The parallel with Paul's conversion on the Damascus Road after the stoning of Stephen is curious.

The odds were too great and the threat to the Eastern Church too dangerous; and Theodora, wife of the Emperor Justinian II, a lady of sanguinary tastes, ordered her agents and troops to scour the cities, mountains and plains of Asia Minor to deal with the heretics. It is said that more than one hundred thousand Paulicians were executed. The Church Militant had a reputation to protect. They did not lay their necks meekly on the block and, in many armed battles, the Paulicians were sometimes victorious. The damage was done and the threat to authority was largely removed. The survivors sought once again, and were granted, the protection of Islam over a period of thirty years.

By the middle of the eighth century they were once more numerous in Constantinople and Thrace; and from this threshold gained entry into Europe proper. The Paulicians were now spoken of in parallel with the Manichaeans who had influenced many heretical sects. In fact, Augustine of Hippo himself was, for nine years, a Manichaean, for it had much common ground with Christianity. They were active in Italy and in France, and West of the Alps in the eleventh and twelfth centuries. They were joined by thousands of pious Catholics sickened by the avarice, despotism and scandalous sexual promiscuity of Popes, Cardinals and other ranks of priesthood. The corruption of the Roman Catholic Church was a disgrace to the memory of Christ.

It was in South West France in the towns near to Albi and in the Languedoc where Nemesis, or perhaps the Devil, finally caught up with the Paulicians now called Cathars and, hence, the Albigensian Heresy. They had regained the purity in spirit, chastity and other virtues that had been the hallmark of Constantine (Sylvanus) and his eighth century followers and it was now the thirteenth century. This so maddened Pope Innocent III he exacted a level of blood thirstiness and cruelty the equal of Theodora. He achieved a level of infamy memorable even for those days and the Cathars were wiped out by the sword and the Inquisition. The soldiers and priests of the Pope did an exemplary job.

The body may have been destroyed, but the spirit of the Paulicians and the Cathars lived on, appearing later in John-Wycliffe in England, and John Huss in Bohemia. Later, three hundred years later, the spirit of the Paulicians was received again by Martin Luther and John Calvin. I fancy Paul and Christ would have felt more at ease with these four than any of the Popes of Rome.

18

THE LEGACY OF PAUL

'I have fought a good fight, I have finished my course,
I have kept the faith.'

The Bible, as sometimes in life, was prone to choose the
second born over the first; or the bad man rather than the
good. Proving, as some might say, there is no justice. Cain
survived over Abel, Isaac was chosen over Ishmael, Jacob
over Esau. God, if you can believe Paul, appointed him in
preference to Peter, the 'first born' of Jesus' Apostles, to
spread Christianity worldwide; or at least Asia Minor wide.
As in modern times Winston Churchill was chosen above
his contemporaries to save civilization from Hitler's
Germany. Cometh the hour, cometh the man. Paul and
Churchill, two men who could see the wood for the trees
and able to observe the target through the fog of indecision,
quarrels and the obscurantism of lesser men.

When Paul went to Rome, what did he leave behind him?
An unknown number of converts in Corinth, Thessalonika,
Antioch in Pisidia, Antioch in Syria. Cyprus, Ephesus,
Derbe, Lystra, Philippi and, one supposes, a few in
Jerusalem. And what did he leave them with in the way of re-
ligious instruction? God is love, have faith in the Risen
Christ, repent your evil ways and all sins will be forgiven.
Become baptised and on death you will go to Heaven. No
matter the crime, the falling by the wayside; repent and you
will be saved. It was so simple, a little child could understand

it. Although I wonder if Paul ever heard Jesus' imprecation 'Suffer little children to come unto me; forbid them not for of such is the Kingdom of God.' Apart from that he left them a set of rules by which he implored them to live; a code of ethics: lust not after the flesh; avoid adultery, fornication, uncleanliness, envy, murder, drunkeness. As commanding as the EXORDIUM in the Koran:

*IN THE NAME OF GOD THE COMPASSIONATE,
THE MERCIFUL
Praise be to God, Lord of the Universe,
The Compassionate, the Merciful,
Sovereign of the Day of Judgement!
You alone we worship, and to You alone we turn for help.
Guide us to the straight path,
The path of those whom You have favoured,
Not of those who have incurred your wrath,
Nor of those who have gone astray.*

But Mahammad and his successors left it there; uncomplicated, from the seventh century to the present day. 'Allah is Great, only believe, study the Koran, obey the simple rules and you will go to Paradise.'

If only Paul had coined the slogan:

'There is no God but God, and Jesus is his Prophet.'

Christianity would have been understood by everybody.

Then it all went pear shaped: what went wrong? With Paul out of the way, some of the clever among the converted must have decided it could not be *that* simple. Gentile converts were probably to blame with their Hellenist background; steeped for generations in metaphysics and magic.

'How', they wondered, 'could a spirit, God himself, be united with a mass of impure contaminated flesh?' They decided to abjure the humanity of God, and over the next two hundred and fifty years the mustard seed, of which Jesus spoke grew to the size of an Amazon rain forest, containing all the horror, evil, corruption and chaos which was the early Christian Church.

Paul then, alas posthumously, had his great stroke of luck. Constantine the Great, after his vision at the Milvian Bridge, of the Cross in the sky giving him victory over his enemies, a gift from the God of the Christians he was sure, appointed in due course Christianity, the Pauline Theology, as the State Religion of the Roman Empire. Without Paul it is surely not unreasonable to believe that his sect, a break-away movement from conventional Judaism, would hardly have moved out of Judea. Especially as Paul had no intention of creating a universal church with a priesthood, tiers of officials, bishops, patriarchs and a veritable circus of bureaucrats. He believed the end of the world would come soon. He spoke of 'Perusia' the Second Coming of Christ within his lifetime. We are, or some of us are, still waiting. Until a few years ago, perhaps even now, it was not uncommon to see an old man walking in the road bearing the sign 'Repent! For the end is Nigh.'.

Constantine, and his father Constantius I, were sympathetic towards the Christian faith and both were also tolerant of the old Pagan Gods. The sign of the Cross, supposedly seen by Constantine at the Milvian Bridge in 312 A.D. *may* have been his apocalypse, as a year later in the Imperial city of Milan the edict, which bears the name of Milan, revoked all previous anti-Christian decrees. He also had a benign attitude towards the soldiers' cult of Mithraism with its sun worship, and it would have been surprising if he did not consider Mithras as a hedge bet because he was very superstitious, like all his forebears. Old habits die hard. Which of us will willingly walk under a ladder? We may consider a black cat lucky but Italians do not. They think quite the reverse. I know an Italian who when he saw a black cat ahead turned round and went home.

Constantine was a cruel man, with a long list of North African massacres to his discredit; who would never have believed in the hymn line 'Gentle Jesus meek and mild.'. Whether his baptism in 330 A.D. shortly before his death convinced him of Christianity's certitudes, or whether he decided it was sound politics to establish Christianity as the new State Religion, it set dramatically the permanent seal on Pauline Theology, which could have died with his death circa 60 A.D. Constantine held neither awe nor excessive respect for bishops or Popes. On the contrary, though they considered their religious authority the gift of God, their temporal or secular powers were at *his* disposal, the Emperor of the Roman Empire. Henry VIII had a similar view on the archbishops and bishops of the Church of England. Constantine had no doubt he was ordained by God, which established his position; and that of all the Emperors and Kings in Europe who followed him. Until in 1649 A.D. when the head of Charles I dropped into the basket.

For generations, hundreds of years even, scholars debated whether Christianity played the whore to the Roman Empire, or did the Empire surrender to Christ and the Christian God? Free from persecution, confident in its relationship to the Crown, the Church created an intricate web of administration, codes of worship, precedence, grand robes, ostentation and outrageous displays of Papal authorityand last, but not least, Canon Law, which ultimately placed itself above Civil Law. In due course, long after Constantine, the Church achieved authority, both religious and secular, before which monarchs were known to tremble in fear of excommunication. Great wealth, drawn from all corners of the known world, found its way to Rome to establish it as the religious, artistic, architectural and intellectual centre of civilization. And it headed, beyond the slightest doubt, the corruption league of civilisation also.

Who, in their wildest dreams, could have imagined that a tent maker could take on the formidable powers of Judaism and set the whole of the Middle East in turmoil? A king maker that in due course would have the whole of Europe kneeling before Christ the King. For without Paul, Jesus of Nazareth, later Christ Crucified and Christ Resurrected, for whom Paul was prepared to be flogged, imprisoned and, ultimately, die, would hardly have been heard of outside of Judea, much less Palestine.

Paul recognised Christ as the visible sign of the Universal God, and he ruthlessly disposed of the pastoral ministry of Jesus, even if he knew much about it, with its firm attachments *still* to Judaism. He forged a religion which had, as its single, simple premise, faith in Christ and the forgiveness of sins. A religion available to all, regardless of rank, colour, wealth or poverty. And that was as it was while Paul and his disciples were proselytising in Antioch, Ephesus, Cyprus, Corinth and many other towns in Asia Minor.

But the Church was more than Rome; in the fourth and fifth centuries Alexandria, Constantinople and Antioch had greater numbers of Christians, and were intellectual and theological hothouses. The source of most of the schisms, Arianism, was the strongest of the creeds, believing that though Christ was divine he was not of the same substance a God. The fact that the people in those three centres preferred the teachings of Arius to Athanasius, the victor of the Council of Nicea, cut little ice with Constantine. He was inclined to take the laissez faire view; live and let live, and mild diversions from the central truth of the Adoration of Christ were alright by him. Confident that the new State Religion was robust and monolithic enough to brush off or absorb the old Pagan worship, and a unifying force for good, he was tolerant also of the Jews, whom he had observed in Rome and Milan as being orderly, obedient and paying their taxes and causing no trouble. If only the Christians were the same, he must have thought.

There was a bonus in Arianism, that could have occurred to nobody. The Gothic hordes that poured across the Danube, from what is now modern Romania, brought Arianism with them. This creed had been embraced by Gothic prisoners of war (slaves) in Constantinople. It was exported back to Romania and brought with the Goths when they invaded Italy, France and Spain.

Paul's task, albeit posthumously, was done. He had converted the Roman Empire, a little untidily perhaps, to the worship of his beloved Saviour. But there was an enigma. His teachings were post Resurrection. At the time of the battle of the Milvian Bridge there had been Christian converts in Rome for two hundred and fifty years or more. But to which brand did they belong? Were they Gentiles of Pagan origin or converts from Judaism like the Jesus Church in Jerusalem, containing the likes of Barnabus and John Mark? Common sense suggests they were mainly Gentiles. In which case they preached Pauline theology and *not* Jesus Nazarine theology.

There is no evidence as to how and when the pastoral teachings of Jesus escaped from Palestine to Rome and other places. If it was by way of Peter and his friends, where is the evidence? His two Epistles, supposedly written from Rome, give no clues; and one of them is considered by the scholars to be a forgery. Eusebius, (R240–300 A.D.), Bishop of Caesarea, says Peter was crucified upside down in Rome in about 60 A.D., based on a year 200 A.D. report by a man called Gaius. What is most likely is that the twenty seven books of the New Testament, written in Greek, including the four Gospels of Matthew, Mark, Luke and John, filtered down to Rome late in the fourth century. Although Jerome (later St. Jerome), a Roman, settled in Bethlehem in 386 A.D. and translated the Bible into Latin (the Vulgate) from the Hebrew. Whichever way it is regarded there were over three hundred years of Pauline theology taught verbally in Rome before the written testimonies of the Nazarines and Jesus their leader arrived. Bearing in mind that the Bible as reading matter was denied to the laity, the church must have been pleased with the written word so easily understood, containing none of the harsh strictures and puritanism of Paulinism.

Full of marvellous stories of miracles done by Jesus, and parables of good and evil so simply written, grateful as the Church was to Paul; grateful as it was to his bringing it to Christ, the Jesus story was unbeatable; it had everything. The descent from Abraham (Matthew), the Virgin Birth and Nativity (Luke and Matthew); the miracles and parables in all four Gospels; the Sermon on the Mount (Matthew); the throwing of the money changers out of the Temple. Then, for the intellectuals, there was the St. John's Gospel with its mysteries. There was something for everybody; and for a people that *still* believed in magic, wanting *still* to hear about miraculous cures as in the days of the Pagan gods. They loved to hear stories of the triumph of good over evil with the bad man getting a jolly good thrashing. By accident, Paul brought all this to the attention of millions yearning for something simple in which to believe.

There is a dark side also to Paul, though I don't think he alone should get the blame for the spreading of the story that the Jews were responsible for the death of Jesus. But is is certain that the persecution of the Jews in Europe dates from the arrival of the Church in Rome *after* it became the State Religion. This resulted in millions of Jews being killed in a variety of ways in every country of what today is called Europe (including Russia), from Russia in the East to Portugal in the West, up to, and in some places beyond, World War II. In retrospect, to me, the story in the Gospels sounds more like Lukespeak than Paul. Reading St. Luke, who is credited with writing the Acts of the Apostles, leaves a deep impression of anti-Semitism.

We are left with a Christian religion that has survived, if shakily, for nearly two thousand years. It has caused tumult, desolation and the destruction of peoples, South and Central America and Mexico are frightening examples. Killing more innocents than guilty, if guilty is the correct word for defending your beliefs and culture. Wars fought purely, though sometimes nominally, in the name of Christ, until the Thirty Years' War (1618–1648). There used to be a famous history question in the days when boys and girls were taught history:

> *'The Thirty Years'War; was it the last of the religious wars, or the first of the Wars of Nationalism? Discuss.'*

Thereafter the nations of the West just went to war: for power, for trade, for territory. Both sides claiming that God was on their side. Should we blame Paul for this also? I think not; man has always been able to justify his murderous and predatory nature, without the need of religious consolation or approval. Let us just say he took on a task greater than the Twelve Tasks of Hercules of the Greek Mythology. What followed was the fault of men, the men of the Church, most of whom were not fit (if I may paraphrase John the Baptist talking of the Son of God), 'to stoop down and unloose the shoes of Paul.'

The Christian churches of the West, save in the U.S.A., are largely empty; its priests and clergymen riven with doubt. The synagogues are full; and the mosques? Ah, the mosques; they overflow onto the sidewalks. And who do the Muslims worship; Paul's God? I think not. The god of the despised Jesus followers, the Nazarines? Perhaps. The God of the Jews, of Abraham, of Moses. Of their semite brethren? I think so. Life is never short of ironies.

Let Paul have the last word:

'Though I speak with the tongues of men and of angels, and have not charity I am become of sounding brass, or a tinkling cymbal. And now abideth faith, hope and charity, these three, and the greatest of these is charity.'

INDEX